Faith in ACTION

GUIDING PRINCIPLES OF THE SALVATION ARMY
SOCIAL SERVICES MINISTRIES

Jim Winship

Social Services Direct Care Handbook
Second Edition

The Salvation Army
USA Central Territory
Commissioner Paul R. Seiler, Territorial Commander
5550 Prairie Stone Parkway
Hoffman Estates, Illinois 60192

Printed in the United States of America.
First edition, 2001. Second edition, 2016.

ISBN: 978-0-9648347-5-0

Designed by Kenneth Romin

For more information on how to obtain resources referenced in this book, contact The Salvation Army Central Territorial Social Services Department USCSocialServiceMail@usc.salvationarmy.org.

Table of Contents

Foreward

The Salvation Army's more than 150-year history of serving the most disenfranchised people in communities throughout the world was initiated by the compassionate spirit of its founder, William Booth. When he learned of men whose only home was under the London Bridge, he ordered his son Bramwell to "Do something!" Since that moment The Salvation Army has been fulfilling its mission "to preach the gospel of Jesus Christ and to meet human needs in His name without discrimination."

The Salvation Army opens its doors daily to respond to individuals who are in crisis—needing material resources, guidance, rehabilitation, emotional, or spiritual care. This is sacred work. It is demanding work. Therefore, Salvation Army officers, soldiers, employees, and volunteers need to be prepared and trained to effectively minister to individuals, families, and communities. Salvation Army personnel serving in direct practice and in supervisory roles need to be equipped to make a positive impact on their work with individuals, families, and communities. Their social work practices must align with The Salvation Army's core values and ethical practice of treating all with dignity.

Therefore, I commend to you *Faith in Action – Social Services Direct Care Handbook, second edition.* I am pleased this resource has been developed to provide guiding principles to assist all personnel who work with individuals and families, regardless of the personnel's formal education and training. This handbook's purpose is to help Salvation Army personnel become more effective in practice within the Army's mission and purposes. The first edition, published in 2001, has been updated in this second edition to include:

- Strengths-based approaches to working with individuals, families, and communities.
- Overview of the Stages of Change Model.
- Incorporation of Motivational Interviewing approaches within casework.
- Strategies and guidance on documenting casework.
- Essential components of developing cultural competence.
- Expanded resources to support the integration of spiritual and emotional care that is built on theories of hope, within ethical practice.
- Case studies that demonstrate our holistic approach to our multiple Salvation Army social services ministries.
- Applications for supervisors and teams in using this handbook to support staff development.

I want to thank the Central Territory Social Services Department for coordinating the development of this revision as a hands-on resource for both the novice and the veteran. We are grateful to the author, the general editors and the Faith in Action Advisory Committee for their contributions. Their expertise helps ensure that Salvation Army personnel are equipped to respond to those who seek a helping hand or listening ear during their immediate life challenge or circumstance.

Each day I am cognizant of and humbled by the trust the public places in The Salvation Army. Although I am grateful for this trust, my heart and mind are more centered on how, as we engage those in need, our work brings glory to God. The practice guidelines and principles in this document are resources for those who desire to serve with compassion and competency. The application of all contained in this handbook begins with you as caseworker or volunteer and your interaction with new participants as they relay their unique story. My hope is that through your daily application of *Faith in Action* and your intentional and purposeful social services approaches, you'll bring the light and hope of the boundless gospel of Jesus Christ.

Paul R. Seiler
Commissioner
Territorial Commander
The Salvation Army
USA Central Territory

Dedication

Faith in Action is dedicated to the men and women who have served God with excellence through the social services ministries of The Salvation Army Central Territory. The following individuals laid the foundation for the innovative programs, social work methods, and ethical practices that affirm the dignity of people we serve.

Lt. Colonel Helen Waara, BS, MA

Lt. Colonel Waara helped pioneer The Salvation Army's social work practices in the Central Territory, serving as an officer from 1929 to 1968. She administered the Chicago Family Services Bureau, the Metropolitan Welfare Department, and the Territorial Social Welfare Department. She received a bachelor of science degree in sociology from Loyola University and a master of arts degree from the University of Chicago—School of Social Service Administration.

Colonel Anita Robb, BS, MSW, OF

Colonel Anita Robb was called at a young age to be a Salvation Army officer, and it was her goal to enter the College for Officer Training already educated and experienced in social services. She attained a bachelor's degree in sociology from Berea College and a master of social work degree from Ohio State University. She collaboratively led the development of guidelines for child care in Illinois and tested those concepts at the Chicago Settlement, which provided numerous services for children and families, integrated with faith-based ministries. Throughout Colonel Robb's officership (1935-1977), she diligently worked to enhance the Army's social work. She was inducted into the Order of the Founder (OF) in 2001.

Lt. Colonel Paul E. Bollwahn, ACSW, CSWM

In his years of officership (1968-2008), Lt. Colonel Bollwahn administered several Salvation Army social services programs and made a significant impact as a leader on territorial and national levels, including serving as the National Social Services Secretary. He is acknowledged for advancing the professional practices of the Army's social services and for his work with collaborating organizations in the United States and abroad. His publication *William Booth: The development of his social concern* highlights the crucial work of social services in The Salvation Army. Lt. Colonel Bollwahn received a bachelor of science degree from Olivet University and a master of social work degree from Jane Adams Graduate School of Social Work and engaged in post graduate work at McCormick Theological Seminary. In 2008 Lt. Colonel Bollwahn received a Life Time Achievement Award from National Association of Social Workers and was acknowledged in 2014 by The Salvation Army's North American Anti-Trafficking Council for his role in starting The Salvation Army response to International Trafficking.

Captain Tom Crocker, OF

The Army's first Harbor Light program opened in Detroit, Michigan, in 1939. Led by several influential officers, the most well-known is "Captain Tom" Crocker. In recovery from his own addiction, he took to the streets around Detroit, ministering to those suffering from alcohol and drug addiction. Becoming a Salvation Army officer two years later, Cadet-Captain Crocker recognized the need to develop a holistic approach to treatment that included life skills classes and addressed the health and mental health needs of those addicted to alcohol and drugs. He served at the Detroit Harbor Light from 1942 to 1948. His integrated model was replicated across the Central Territory and, through his national leadership, branched out to The Salvation Army's Southern and Western territories, resulting in thousands of men and women finding freedom from substance abuse. In 1952, then Senior-Captain Crocker was inducted into the Order of the Founder and honored as Chicagoan of the Year.

Acknowledgements

About the Author

Jim Winship, MSW, PhD., is Professor of Social Work at the University of Wisconsin-Whitewater and has been a Fulbright Scholar in El Salvador and Colombia. He has provided training for Salvation Army social services personnel for several decades and authored the first edition of *Faith in Action* in 2001.

***Faith in Action* General Editors**

Maribeth Velazquez Swanson, MSW
Territorial Social Services Secretary

Susan Spreiter, MSW
Territorial Program Consultant—Evaluation Coordinator

***Faith in Action* Contributors**

We wish to thank the *Faith in Action* Advisory Committee for their significant contributions in planning, researching, writing, and editing this handbook:

Linda Brinker, MSW
Territorial Pathway of Hope Project Manager

Helen Campbell, MA
Territorial Youth and Children Services Consultant

Bryant Erickson, MSW
Territorial Social Services Program Consultant

LaKeysha Fields, MSW
Midland Division Pathway of Hope Regional Coordinator

Alfredo Martinez, MDiv
Territorial Hispanic Ministries Consultant

Major Arnel Ruppel, MNA
Adult Rehabilitation Center Command Secretary for Program

Susan Solmon, MA
Indiana Division Social Services Director

Sherrie Trucker, MA
Northern Division Pathway of Hope Regional Coordinator

Karen Young, MA
Territorial Multicultural Ministries Specialist

Also, we extend our many thanks to the divisions and programs that contributed their stories and case studies to the practical applications of this book.

PART I

Foreward and Framework

CHAPTER 1

Introduction to The Salvation Army Social Services

Individuals just hired to work in The Salvation Army Social Services may initially be struck by things very different from other social services organizations—the uniforms, the military titles of leaders of the organization and, in many cases, a chapel in the building where they work. What they come to realize is they are working for an organization that has had the dual mission of compassionate care and Christian ministry for over 150 years.

William Booth, founder of The Salvation Army was born April 10, 1829, in Nottingham, England. He was forced to leave school at age 13 to help financially support his family by becoming an apprentice in a pawnbroker shop. Booth's compassion for the poor was influenced not only by his family's own deprivation. He also was exposed to the desperation of those who came into the shop to sell their most precious and utilitarian items.

At age 15, William Booth gave his heart to God through a dramatic conversion experience in the Methodist church, resolving to serve God by following Jesus. By age 35 he had become an itinerant evangelist. Highly regarded for his fervent oratory and passionate preaching, he was asked to fill in one night for an ill preacher during evangelistic meetings in the East End of London. "Inside the closed canvas walls the air was heavy with a mixture of drunken vapors and noxious odors from the naphtha lamps.... Those who came were unkempt, amid the poorest in the spiritual wilderness known as London's Mile End.... Upon returning that evening to his home he pronounced to his wife Catherine, 'O, Kate, I have found my destiny'" (Gariepy, 2009, p. 7).

By1865 that destiny became reality with the founding of The Christian Mission, which evolved into The Salvation Army in 1878. When Booth founded The Christian Mission, it was for the purpose of saving souls. He did not emphasize "social redemption." On one occasion he said, "My brethren, my comrades, soul saving is our avocation, the great purpose of our lives. Let us be Salvationists indeed!" (Booth, n.d., p. 19).

However, in his work in the slums of London, he was greatly affected by the poverty and wretched conditions. In 1869, he wrote:

> Day by day the mass of pauperism is being intensified. Hunger and misery reign supreme in the homes of the poor.... sickness and fever tread closely on heels of want, and in the thin, pinched features of many a little one, in their wasted arms and shrunken heads, we read the sad story of parental privation and suffering. Another danger is springing up. Large numbers of young women, usually employed in the manufacture of articles of clothing, find themselves deprived of work and, having no friends or resources, are being helplessly driven into a life of shame and misery. All the poverty of the metropolis, together with no small proportion of that from the provinces, seems steadily gravitating towards East London.

Booth's vision grew to include meeting the needs of the total person. According to him, "A citadel is not only a house of prayer, but a center of every humanizing and spiritualizing influence and activity." He also wrote, "I saw that when the Bible said, 'He that believeth shall be saved,' it meant not only saved from the miseries of the future world but from the miseries of this also—that it came with the promise of salvation here and now; from hell and sin and vice and crime and idleness and extravagance and consequently very largely from poverty and disease, and the majority of kindred foes."

Booth originally had no intention of developing a denomination. He thought if he could convert the poor, they would then find their place in the surrounding churches. However, the churches did not want his recovering alcoholics, reformed prostitutes, or unruly children. He and his wife were then thrown into developing an organizational structure and in training their new converts to assist in supporting the growing ministry.

In 1890, with the editorial assistance of journalist W.T. Stead, Booth published *In Darkest England and the Way Out.* In this book, Booth laid out his comprehensive plan for serving the poor, the homeless, those without jobs, criminals, and lost children. He challenged British politicians and the public to wake up and see the "Submerged Tenth" (p. 24), the estimated ten percent that lived in "destitution and despair" (p. 31). Booth exhorted:

> Who are the Lost? I reply, not in a religious, but in a social sense, the lost are those who have lost their foothold in Society, those to whom the prayer to our Heavenly Father: "Give us this day our daily bread" is either unfulfilled, or only fulfilled by the Devil's wages, by the earning of vice, the proceeds of crime, or the contribution enforced by the threat of the law (p. 25).

The militaristic aspects of The Salvation Army—its organizational structure with military titles and uniforms—were developed within the context of the power (and positive image) of the military strength of the British Empire in the late 1800s. Green (2005) notes that Booth was able to capitalize on the military language and imagery of the day that showed The Salvation Army as a force that rescued the down-and-out from eternal and social hell. In addition, this imagery appealed to the well-to-do who were fascinated by Booth's Army.

By 1889, William Booth had officially established his twofold ministry—personal salvation and social salvation (Green, 2005). As Booth's theology and mission evolved, he was moved to establish social programs focused on social redemption: "Why all this apparatus of temples and meetinghouses to save men from perdition in a world which is to come, while never a helping hand is stretched out to save them from the inferno of their present life?" (Booth, 1890, p. 23). Booth embraced John Wesley's teaching: "the gospel of Christ knows no religion, but social; no holiness but social holiness." This Wesleyan thought influenced Booth's own theological evolution (Green, 1989, p.101) that continues to permeate the Army's mission and structure to this day—Christian faith is to be lived in relationship to other believers and the church. God's love is the source of service and action.

The proceeds from *In Darkest England and the Way Out* supported Booth's expanded ministry. Booth and his young Army assessed the appalling working conditions, meager wages, and the dozen of cases of phosphorus necrosis, or "phossy jaw"—a facial disfigurement that resulted from working in match factories with white phosphorous (Gariepy, 2009). Booth put his practical religion to work in 1891 when he opened up a match factory. The factory employed one hundred girls and used only safe red phosphorus; it paid an adequate living wage, much higher than the pay of the for-profit factories (Gariepy, 2009).

In his book *In Darkest England and the Way Out,* Booth outlined his seven "Essentials to Success" that demonstrated his understanding of oppression and continues to inform The Salvation Army's service philosophy and approach to social action. Although written in the language of his time, the strength and compassion-based philosophy of the Army's social services are evident in these principles:

1) To be effectual, it must change the circumstances of the individual when they are the cause of his wretched condition and lie beyond his control.
2) It must be on a scale commensurate with the evil with which it proposes to deal. It is no use trying to bail out the ocean with a pint pot.
3) Not only must the Scheme be large enough, but it must be permanent. That is, it must not be merely a sporadic effort.
4) It must also be immediately practicable.
5) The indirect features of the Scheme must not be such as to produce injury to the persons who we seek to benefit.
6) While assisting one class of the community, it must not seriously interfere with the interests of another (1890, pp. 93-95).
7) Effective intervention must include strategies that alter social circumstances and outside forces as they contribute to suffering (1890, p. 95). (This commitment to Social Justice is discussed in Chapter 12)

Conclusion

The Salvation Army ranks as one of the largest international social and relief organizations.

What was begun by William Booth to meet the total needs of individuals has grown and spread throughout the world in the past century and a half. Today, The Salvation Army ranks as one of the largest international social and relief organizations, officially established in 127 countries and working unofficially in others, and serves people in 175 languages. In the United States, the Army is organized into four territories: East, South, West, and Central. Eleven Midwest states encompass the Central Territory.

Reflection questions

1. On page 5 it states: "The militaristic aspects of The Salvation Army—its organizational structure with military titles and uniforms—were developed within the context of the power (and positive image) of the military strength of the British Empire in the late 1800s." Are there imagery and message, in your opinion, The Salvation Army could use that would appeal to today's society?
2. On page 6 is William Booth's Seven Essentials for Success. Which of these do you think are most relevant to the work of The Salvation Army today? Why?

CHAPTER 2

Faith, Religion, Spirituality, and Social Services

Social services in The Salvation Army cannot be examined without discussing the roles of faith, religion, and spirituality. In The Salvation Army Social Services Code of Ethics (Appendix A), the first point under Responsibility to Participants is that personnel will: "Reflect in their practice the high value of each individual conferred by their Creator-God. Reflect in their practice that The Salvation Army exists for those it meets in ministry and seeks to influence the world towards the betterment of humankind."

This chapter presents definitions of faith, religion, and spirituality and discusses positive outcomes associated with them. It shows the relationship between the profession of social work and the Army and demonstrates ways spiritual and religious dynamics are integrated into the Army's social services.

Definitions of faith, religion, and spirituality

Having faith involves trusting that one's belief in the ultimate meaning in the universe is true. While faith often is associated with a religious tradition, it is deeper, richer, and more personal:

> It is an orientation of the personality, to oneself, to one's neighbors, to the universe; a total response; a way of seeing what-

ever one sees, and of handling whatever one handles; a capacity to live at more than a mundane level; to see, to feel, to act in terms of a transcendent dimension (Smith, 1979).

Although the terms "spirituality" and "religion" are often used interchangeably, the words differ in important ways. Spirituality can be seen as a set of personal beliefs that come from an individual's perception of self and his or her relationship to the natural world and to some world or reality beyond what can be seen. As individuals try to understand the meaning and purpose of life, they often seek answers from a higher power in comprehending the sources of belonging and isolation, faith and doubt, hope and despair, suffering and joy (Graham, Kaiser, and Garrett, 1998).

Unlike spirituality, where individual spiritual experiences can take place without a structured belief system, religions have beliefs and moral codes that their members generally share. Hodge defines religion as: "a particular set of beliefs, practices, and rituals that has been developed in community by people who share similar existential experiences of transcendent reality" (2001, p. 36).

Positive outcomes associated with religion and spirituality

In many ways people's religious beliefs and practices are strengths. Members of faith communities often find support in times of trouble, for example when Christians live out Galatians 6:2, "Bear ye one another's burdens, and so fulfill the law of Christ" (KJV).

A growing body of scientific research indicates that spirituality and religion are important assets in contributing to a range of social, physical, and mental health well-being and promoting and sustaining positive changes in individuals (Koenig, King, and Carson, 2012).

One example of this comes from a study (Hong, 2012) in which a sample of low-income job seekers participating in an employment program were administered a series of tests: the Intrinsic Spirituality Scale (Hodge, 2003), the Hope Scale (Snyder, *et al.,* 1991), and the WEN Economic Self-Sufficiency Scale (ESS) (Gowdy & Pearlmutter, 1993). The results indicated that increased spirituality was correlated with the belief one could achieve the desired results, which then led to increased self-sufficiency. Thus, there appears to be a strong connection between belief in one's capacity to meet one's goals and the capacity of individuals to achieve self-sufficiency.

Persons from marginalized groups and those who face barriers beyond their personal and community resources often rely on and benefit from community social support, their faith, and their belief that the Divine is with them and acting on their behalf (Snyder, Rand, and Sigmon, 2002). As St. Paul wrote, "I can do all things through Christ which strengtheneth me" (Philippians 4:13, KJV). This infuses confidence and self-worth (agency) in believers that they have the capacity to accomplish their goals.

Relationship between the profession of social work and faith, religion, and spirituality

Social work as a profession began in the 1870s when non-governmental organizations such as Charity Organization Societies and settlement houses began to hire paid staff. The amount of work was becoming too great for volunteers alone to carry out. Many of the earliest social workers saw the work as a way to express their faith. Additionally, social work originated from the Judeo-Christian religious traditions of its philanthropic founders. However, by the 1890s, the gap between professional social work and the social ministry of churches was widening for a variety of reasons. Some evangelical ministers, such as Billy Sunday and Dwight Moody, opposed church-related and secular social work services. Their perception was that the services detracted from the primary mission of saving souls (Loewenberg, 1988).

From the perspective of the newly formed profession of social work, there were reasons to move away from being identified with religion. In order to increase the credibility of the profession, social workers wanting to be seen as more than "do-gooders" looked to science and the promise of objectivity. Social workers found that religious sources did not provide them with the desired scientific theory base, so they abandoned religion and turned instead to other sources, principally to psychological and sociological theories.

Social workers also thought that by distancing themselves from religion, spirituality, and churches they would "avoid being considered similar to less-skilled clergy, avoid the possibility of contributing to religious institutional oppression, and avoid the appearance of proselytizing or otherwise imposing values on participants" (Graham, Kaiser, and Garrett, 1998).

The gulf between social work and religion/spirituality persisted until recent decades. Some social workers believed the Constitutional separation between church and state prohibited them from mentioning anything religious. Many social workers accepted the principle of separating church and state in their professional lives as in government. Even when they sought answers or reassurances from religious sources in their personal life, they often saw religion as having relatively little bearing on their professional lives. Perhaps the most common reasons social workers did not address spiritual issues were their discomfort with entering the spiritual arena or a lack of confidence in their abilities to work with participants around spiritual issues.

The Council on Social Work Education, which oversees the teaching of social work in the USA, now emphasizes the inclusion of material on religion and spirituality in social work education programs. With its inclusion, students develop approaches and skills for working with participants of different faiths and spiritual backgrounds. The Code of Ethics of the National Association for Social Workers (NASW) states that social workers should show respect for the religious beliefs of their participants, should not discriminate on the basis of religion, and should not engage in social and political action that would exploit or discriminate against any religion (National Association for Social Workers, 2006). NASW Standards for Social Work Case Management (National Association for Social Workers, 2013) state that workers should be aware of the role of spirituality in participants' (and their own) cultural identification and how this influences beliefs and actions.

Integration of faith, religion, and spirituality

The Salvation Army's social services are integrated into its holistic ministry as part of its mission "to preach the gospel of Jesus Christ and to meet human needs in His name without discrimination." Mission statements, however, mean little unless they are visible in the life of an organization. Ways the Army's mission is alive in its social services work include the ministry of presence, being open to the spiritual aspects of human need, helping those suffering from trauma make sense of the world, and connecting participants with Pastoral Care (see Chapter 12).

Ministry of presence

All Salvation Army social services are religious in that they can be seen as carrying out the will of Jesus Christ. Lt. Colonel Paul Bollwahn, former National Social Services Secretary, stated, "It is our view that all social casework rendered through an organization like ours, committed to Christ and His gospel, while perhaps not 'soul-saving' in and of itself, is redemptive because of its nature and setting. It is what we call 'presence evangelism.'"

When persons coming to The Salvation Army for material assistance or for other services experience a helping environment in which they are treated with dignity and as important persons by Salvation Army officers and staff, they experience the *ministry of presence.* This can be valuable, as Gordon Bingham, former Western Territorial Social Services Secretary, stated:

> Those we serve (in) emergency assistance are hurting, frustrated, understandably angry people. If we offer them a service that is loving, sensitive to their hurt, that does not seek to impose our agenda, but responds to their own, I think we will in many instances find opportunity in other ways to address those issues that go beyond today's survival. If we do not, I think we only confirm them in their cynicism and alienation (1989, p. 16).

Edward Kuhlmann, former Executive Director of the North American Association of Christians in Social Work, expressed it this way: "Social workers, regardless of their own awareness, are God's representatives in creation and as such cooperate with God in providing for the well-being of others" (1999, p. 36).

The Salvation Army recognizes that not all of its employees engaged in providing its social services programs are professing Christians. Yet, as long as all workers can practice within the Army's mission and values, individuals assisted may experience the love of God, even if that is not the intent of the worker. This is the power of the practice of presence and practical ministry.

Being open to the spiritual aspects of human need

When one is working on more than just meeting material assistance needs, workers may also pay attention to other concerns. Participants may not recognize spiritual issues at all, yet spiritual issues may be central to a participant's crisis—or life. If workers are not sensitive to the spiritual dimensions of people's lives, they may be missing important keys to understanding and effective action. The phrase "I wouldn't have seen it if I hadn't believed it" is applicable here. Workers may not see or hear important parts of participants' lives if they do not believe that religion and spirituality are important. Some people come to The Salvation Army for help because it is a church, and they expect that the spiritual aspects of their situations will be attended to.

Helping individuals suffering from trauma make sense of the world

Religion and spirituality can help make sense of a flawed world when individuals have been uprooted by a natural disaster, suffered violence, experienced the unexpected loss of someone close to them, or been affected by some other personal tragedy. When people experience traumatic life events, their fundamental assumptions about the safety of the world, their beliefs in a Creator, and their view of themselves can be shattered or at least shaken (Locke, Garrison, and Winship, 1998).

Herman (1992) suggests that trauma challenges one to be a theologian, to ask "big picture" questions when experiences change our perception of the world. Alice Seabold testified to this loss of security: "When I was raped, I lost my virginity and almost lost my life. I also discarded certain assumptions I had held about how the world worked and about how safe I was" (page 50).

Combat veterans, who saw things (and did things) on the battlefield that most of us only encounter watching movies or in nightmares, often have trouble reconciling their experiences with the faith in which they grew up. For many young soldiers, their battlefield experience shattered their conceptions of right and wrong, and the exposure to evil resulted in strong feelings of shame and guilt. After returning, many combat veterans are engaging in spiritual practices to promote their healing (Harris, *et al.,* 2011).

Individuals react in different ways to traumatic events. While studies show that 50-90 percent of the population have experienced a traumatic event, only 9 percent have suffered PTSD (the highest risk, 50 percent, was associated with torture or kidnapping). Based on survivors of Nazi concentration camps who were able to maintain good health and a good life after their horrific experiences, the researcher Aaron Antonovosky developed the concept of "sense of coherence" (SOC). SOC is based on three components—how comprehensible, meaningful, and manageable life is. Religious beliefs and spiritual practices can help individuals recovering from traumatic events find meaning and make sense of the world (Peres, *et al.,* 2006).

Christian faith in practice

Alan Keith-Lucas stated: "What we can do as social workers—and we have a wonderful opportunity to do so—is show such love and forgiveness that a confused and desperate person can understand the Spirit's message when it comes" (1985, p. 28).

There may be specific ways in which one's faith and beliefs can be used in social services work. Under some circumstances it may be appropriate to pray with participants. This is fitting when the participants have made it clear their Christian faith is an important part of their life, or if they are seeking spiritual guidance and requesting prayer. The following, reprinted with permission from *Social Work and Christianity,* discusses these issues and highlights the productive use of prayer with participants:

> The relationship between the participant's faith and the social worker's faith is expressed, either implicitly or explicitly, as the meaning of life events is discussed, as goals and objectives are agreed upon in the professional contract, and as values and beliefs influence the shared work. One of the most controversial expressions of shared faith in the social work relationship involves the use of prayer. Prayer is "orientation towards God," bodily and mentally stretching forth to God (Farnsworth, 1981, p. 70). Whether spoken or not, prayer is communication with the Holy Other. As communication, prayer pulls another—God—into the relationship between social worker and participant, whether the participant is an individual, family, or group.
>
> The content and context of prayer is cultural. Prayer is formed in the language of persons, and language is an expression of culture. The order and arrangement of thoughts, as well as the concern for issues and need for quiet waiting, derive from the cultural context. Prayer also provides a route for the Spirit to break into our cultural context. Prayer with another person, then, is often a cross-cultural process. I need to know the participant's understanding of prayer and its meaning before I launch into a prayer that may frighten, alienate, or anger the participant. I need also to be clear about my objectives in praying. Prayer can be used productively:
>
> 1) To frame my work as incomplete and flawed. Often we need to make explicit our sense of failure or inadequacy, to ourselves, to God—and to our participant. When we place our work in the hands of God, asking for guidance and presence, we step down from a position of control. In some respects, this resembles taking a one-down position, as described by strategic therapists, as a means of moving beyond the struggle for

control with a resistant participant (Everstine and Everstine, 1983; Fisch, Weakland, and Segal, 1983).

2) To "center" our work with the participant in the purpose and meaning of the participant's life. Often a time of prayer together helps frame the issue being confronted within the entire life situation of the participant. Prayer confronts a participant and worker with the spiritual significance of the issue at hand. Prayer can help them gain a perspective that, as important as the problem may be, it may not be ultimate. Prayer leads them to reframe a problem as one aspect of life, not all of life. In addition to dealing with problems through intervention to erase them, participants sometimes need to learn to live with chronic problems. This kind of prayer is not intended to minimize the problem, but to support participants as they search for a context of meaning for the problem.

3) To identify the participant's spiritual self, or the spiritual relationship between the persons of a multi-person participant system. Sprenkle describes his work with a sex addict, a deeply committed Christian, and the importance of joining the framework of his faith by beginning and ending sessions with prayer and identifying himself as "an agent of God's healing love" (1987, p. 13). A participant's trust in a shared faith makes possible discussion of difficult value-laden issues, and prayer can provide a foundation for such sharing.

4) To claim the promises of God and generate hope. Those promises may be for forgiveness and redemption, for peace, for God's presence with us.

5) To teach prayer. When the disciples asked Jesus to teach them to pray, he taught them by praying. Likewise, as a spiritual guide the worker may use prayer as a direct intervention in the spiritual dimension of the participant's life. The worker may model ways to pray, to meditate, to use the prayers of others.

In contrast, there are several inappropriate objectives for prayer.

Prayer should not be used to exert influence over the other, either during prayer ("God, help this poor soul to choose sobriety") or after ("I think God would have you do it this way"). Prayer should not be used as a way to prove the social worker's spirituality to the participant—this should be apparent in all relationships. Prayer should not be used as an escape when the worker does not know what to say, although the worker may find prayer useful when the participant and worker are experiencing together a need to know where to turn (Garland, 1991, pp. 85-87).

Conclusion

The integration of faith and practice IS effective practice.

When human needs are met with caring and dignity, the participant's whole being is touched. When practice goes beyond meeting basic human needs and progresses to healing and transformation, the religious and spiritual aspects of people also are involved.

Workers need to understand the belief systems of those with whom they work. "To work with 'the person in the environment,' the worker must include the participant's interpretation of the environment" (Pellebon and Anderson, 1999, p. 32). To be sensitive to the religious and spiritual beliefs of participants is to be culturally sensitive, for in some cases religious beliefs are critical to the person's understanding of the world and their place in it.

When workers are aware of the diversity of spiritual backgrounds and of churches, temples, faith-based support groups, and other spiritual resources, they are more fully meeting the needs of those they serve.

There need not be a distinction between effective practice and practice open to spirituality and religion. Jon Wallace (1998) described the integration of the National Association of Social Workers Code of Ethics and the teaching of Jesus Christ (in italics):

According to the NASW Code of Ethics, the primary mission of the social work profession is to enhance human well-being and to help meet the basic human needs of all people, *for I was hungry and you gave Me food; I was thirsty and you gave Me drink,* with particular attention to needs and empowerment of people who are vulnerable, oppressed, and living in poverty. *I was naked and you clothed Me; I was sick and you visited Me.* A historic and defining feature of social work is the profession's focus on individual well-being in a social context and the well-being of society. *I was a stranger and you took Me in.* Fundamental to social work is attention to the environmental forces that create, contribute to, and address problems in living. *I was in prison and you came to Me* (this relates to the goals of social work). *And the King will answer and say to them, Assuredly, I say to you, inasmuch as you did it to one of the least of these my brethren, you did it to Me* (Matthew 25:35-36, 40, NKJV).

Reflection questions

1) On page 10 it states: "A growing body of scientific research indicates that spirituality and religion are important assets in contributing to a range of social, physical, and mental health well-being and promoting and sustaining positive changes in individuals." In what situations have you seen the spirituality and religion of individuals contributing to their well-being?

2) On page 13 it states: "When one is working on more than just meeting material assistance needs, workers may also pay attention to other concerns. Participants may not recognize spiritual issues at all, yet spiritual issues may be central to a participant's crisis—or life." In what situations have you seen spiritual issues as central to a participant's crisis or life?

CHAPTER 3

Practicing at the Intersection of the Legal Framework, Values, and Ethics

In providing effective social services, workers need to realize the complexity not only of the situation the individual or family presents but also of a number of interrelated factors. One needs to take into account the legal framework of services, the legal status of individuals, one's own values and morals, The Salvation Army's Social Services Code of Ethics, and values important to the Army's social services—hope, dignity, self-determination, and the strengths perspective.

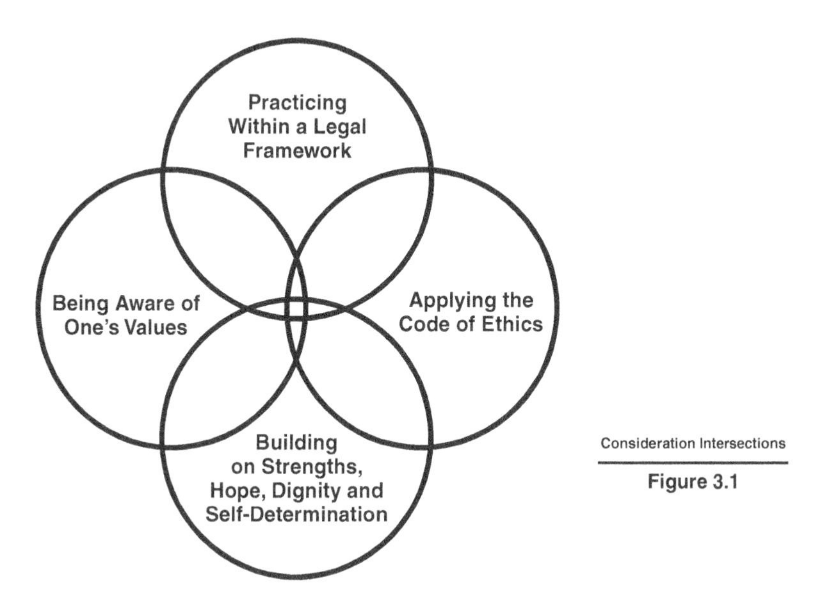

Consideration Intersections

Figure 3.1

Legal Framework

Participants seeking help from The Salvation Army often receive or are seeking help from government agencies and programs and may be unclear or misinformed regarding the legal requirements and regulations of those programs. It has been said "the devil is in the details," and understanding the differing requirements between programs is essential in order to provide effective help to participants. For example, the asset limits (how much money a participant can have and still qualify for services) are different for TANF (Temporary Assistance for Needy Families) programs, Supplemental Security Income (SSI), and subsidized housing.

The requirements for workers who are certified or licensed professionals also vary by state and type of services. An illustration of this comes from legislation related to elder abuse. State laws vary widely on the definitions of elderly and abuse—whether the abuse is a criminal or civil offense, the sanctions or penalties for the abuse, and who is required to report suspected instances of abuse (Stiegel, 1995). One Iowa legislator promoting changes in that state's elder abuse laws stated: "The system currently is a patchwork of laws and responses that won't be improved by merely adding more patches" (Boshart, 2013). Supervisors and workers need to be aware of changes in state and federal laws, and workers who move from one state to another should not assume the laws will be the same.

Workers also need to be knowledgeable about laws that concern those in the United States without permission. Approximately 11 million people in the United States are unauthorized or undocumented, and nine million of these live in "mixed-status" families, where at least one person in the family has legal status in the U.S. and at least one person is undocumented (Pew Hispanic Center, 2013). Workers encounter many situations in which at least one child in a family, born in the United States, is eligible for government services or benefits and others are not. Although undocumented individuals are not eligible for government services and benefits, workers need to know what organizations in their area help individuals and families regardless of their immigration status.

Being aware of our personal values and morals

We all are products of our individual backgrounds and our own experiences. From our families we acquired ideas about morality and principles concerning the distinction between right and wrong and between good and bad behavior. We all value some behaviors and beliefs more than others. For many couples, giving children opportunities to develop their talents as they grow up is a top priority. Based on this value, these parents make decisions about where to put time and discretionary income. However, if a worker who values this in her personal life judges other families using this standard—"they're not child-centered"—then she is imposing her values on them.

Essential values: Dignity, self-determination, hope, and strengths perspective

These essential values will be discussed in this section. In The Salvation Army Social Services Code of Ethics, the fourth principle is: "Respect the human dignity, civil and legal rights, right to self-determination, and right to informed consent of participants."

Dignity

Respecting the dignity of all who come to The Salvation Army for social services is perhaps the most central value. Dignity has three components: the intrinsic worth of all people, the person's view of self and the actions that reflect that intrinsic worth, and the way others respond to the person. People have a basic human right to be *treated equally* regardless of their place in life or their actions. According to Seltser and Miller (1993), "[t]here is a surprising consensus in our religious and philosophical traditions concerning a dignity in human life that is independent of any of the vagaries or accidents of social standing or personal action. There is an inner worth that is to be acknowledged, respected, and acted upon" (p. 95).

To be treated equally before the law does not by itself ensure that one is treated with dignity. To be seen as a person of worth is first and foremost to be seen as a person, not just a member of a racial or ethnic group and not defined by a label or a stereotype. We do not want to be thought of as "just" workers, and we do not like it when others use a single fact such as our gender, race, or occupation to define us. When people acknowledge that a number of things make a worker who he or she is, they are treating him or her with the dignity the person deserves.

Intrinsic worth is an abstraction. It becomes internalized when people carry themselves with dignity and act in ways that show they consider themselves to be of value and are worthy of recognition and acknowledgment. It is possible to claim we have dignity even if no one else treats us with dignity. But the term is social and psychological as well as philosophical. In reality, it would be hard to act with dignity if no one else affirmed this. Both conditions are required: we carry ourselves with dignity, and other people respond to us (or should respond to us) as people with dignity (Seltser and Miller, 1993).

These authors add that people deserve to be related to in a manner that allows them to have an inner attitude, a world of dreams and hopes, and intentions towards the future. To attack the dignity of others is to treat them as if they merely mirror their circumstances, as if they accept others' interpretations of their lives and are subject to other peoples' agendas (p. 93). Indeed, in those situations in which individuals do not treat themselves with dignity, it may be even more important to interact with them in ways that communicate we see them as important persons.

In working with individuals experiencing being homeless, for example, we need to be aware of how hard it is to hold onto one's dignity when homeless. Staff who work with men who are single and homeless report that it is common for these men to lose their driver's licenses or other forms of ID. There are few places in shelters to safely leave their possessions, and in moving from place to place, they may lose things, leave them behind, or have them stolen. The longer people have been on the streets, have been disenfranchised, the less important the ID (literally, their identity) becomes to them (Locke, Garrison, and Winship, 1998).

A social worker who worked with homeless families for a period of time stated:

> Often I heard expressions of guilt at being homeless, as not being able to provide a roof over their own heads and those of their children, assault their own sense of identity as "good" parents. It also seemed that, even more than other low-income parents in parenting groups or classes I had led, these parents initially opposed the idea there was anything about their parenting that could use improvement. I came to realize their primary identity was in being a parent. Their jobs were usually low paying and insecure, and most of the women were not in permanent, stable relationships. Their identity was largely in their relationship with their children, and to admit they could be doing a better job parenting was to weaken their one core identity (Winship, 2014).

One simple way in which we treat people with dignity is by appropriately addressing them. Addressing a participant as Mr., Mrs., or Ms. is a sign of respect. This can especially be an issue for some African-Americans when some white people call them by their first names regardless of their age. Also, in many Latin cultures it is impolite to refer to a person by their first name unless he or she is a family member, friend, or acquaintance. One way to be certain the worker is not unintentionally being disrespectful is to always call all adults by their title (such as Mr.) and their last name. Generally, if individuals prefer workers to use their first name, they will let them know.

In working with people over a period of time, make an effort to remember details from their life from one session to another. Asking a woman about the health of her daughter (when the daughter had an earache the last time the worker saw her) communicates to the participant she is important enough that the worker remembers important details of her life. After all, we remember those life details for other people we care about—family members and good friends.

We also can emphasize the options participants have, the choices they can make. Even when a person's choices are limited, it is important to help them see there is a degree of control and agency in deciding how to take the next step.

Finally, we can apply the verse Luke 6:31 (MEV) from the New Testament, "Do unto others as you would have them do unto you." This sentiment is found in most major religions. When we workers treat participants with the same kind of respect and dignity that we appreciate being treated, participants will see they are being recognized as people of value.

Self-determination

Few people would argue against respecting the dignity of another person. However, participant self-determination seems to be less of a straightforward good. As applied to case management, it refers to the participants' right to determine the form, direction, and substance of the case management help they receive (Rapp, 1998). Participants' choices of goals and ways of meeting those goals are to be respected.

The reality is that people have choices. Some decisions, such as to get help or to change aspects of one's life, require the commitment of the person(s) involved, or nothing will happen (Rothman, 1989). The term "resistant" is often applied to participants who do not show up for appointments, take medications, or carry out tasks specified by the worker. At times, this may be due to the participants' not seeing value in the appointment, medication, or task. It also may be that not showing up or refusing to do what is required is the only power the participants have. Doing nothing or "dragging their heels" is the only opportunity they see to make choices. From Motivational Interviewing comes the idea it is important to think of statements participants make as to why they cannot make changes as "sustain talk"—that is, the statements are in the service of holding on to current habits or ways of doing things. This reframing helps us realize participants may be voicing their desire for, need for, and/or positive benefits of the status quo (Rosengren, 2009).

Fostering the self-determination of participants is important from a competency-building perspective. We want to aid participants in living as independently as possible and to rely on themselves and naturally occurring resources as much as possible. Making choices and learning how to implement and live with them is a necessary part of becoming more independent.

Strengths-based case management programs strive to move each participant to the center of the decision-making process. The worker works on behalf of the participant, involving the participant in every decision. This involvement is based on the premise the work is a collaborative effort, that participants know better than others what they want, but they often need help figuring out how to reach those goals (Rapp, 1998).

Studies of case management in welfare-to-work programs are showing that giving participants choices and establishing trust in an ongoing relationship are necessary to achieve permanent changes in their behavior (Hagen and Davis, 1995, Wagner and Herr, 1995). In a study of case management with welfare-to-work participants in Tennessee, almost 200 workers identified characteristics of effective workers. "Commitment to the participants' rights to direct their own lives" was seen as the most important element (Bricker-Jenkins, 1992).

Self-determination becomes an issue when it conflicts with other values. In many cases, there can be a dilemma between a participant's right to act in ways that may be personally destructive and a worker's obligation to prevent harm to the participant and/or to others (Reamer, 1993).

How then do we react when participants are behaving in ways that appear not to be in their own self-interest? When their actions threaten the well-being of others, we must intervene. When individuals threaten to kill themselves or others, the police need to be informed. When a person's self-destructive actions can best be described as "long-term suicidal behavior," the imperative to act is less clear.

Attempting to force people to take paths they do not want to follow rarely works. What we can do is demonstrate our caring, point out options less dangerous, and maintain relationships with them. We can work with them in the hope their idea of what they want to do with their life will change. We can build on and build up hope.

Hope

For many individuals seeking help at The Salvation Army, their immediate troubles are not their only liability. They often lack hope. This is not to say they are by nature pessimists, expecting the worst. It's just that life has not been good for a long time, and the idea of things getting better just doesn't seem possible to them. Many people seem locked in "an eternal present," where they don't believe deep down things will really get better. Despair is too often their daily lot.

When people lack hope, they are without one of their strongest allies. Viktor Frankl survived a Nazi concentration camp during World War II and used those experiences to explain: "The prisoner who had lost faith in the future—his future—was doomed. With his loss of faith in the future, he had lost his spiritual hold; he let himself decline and became subject to mental and physical decay" (Frankl, 1963, p.117). He quoted Nietzsche, "'He who has a why to live for can bear almost any how.' In the Nazi concentration camps, he noticed those who knew there was a task waiting for them to fulfill were most apt to survive" (Frankl, 1963, pp. 164-165).

A sense of hope can be powerful, but as a concept it is hard to define. *Merriam-Webster* dictionary gives these three definitions of hope:

1) The feeling of wanting something to happen and thinking that it could happen; a feeling that something good will happen or be true.
2) The chance that something good will happen.
3) Someone or something that may be able to provide help—someone or something that gives a reason for hoping.

Definitions of hope are coming out of social science research. The Herth Hope Scale, one of the assessment measures used in the Army's Pathway of Hope approach*, uses this definition: "A multidimensional dynamic life force characterized by a confident yet uncertain expectation of achieving good, which, to the hoping person, is realistically possible and personally significant" (Dufault and Martocchio, 1985. p. 380).

In research using the Herth Hope Scale, the three dimensions of hope that were confirmed through factor analysis were:

1) Temporary and Future: represents the cognitive-temporal dimension of the model (the perception that a positive, desired outcome is realistically probable in the near or distant future).
2) Positive Readiness and Expectancy: represents the affective-behavioral dimension (a feeling of confidence with initiation of plans to affect the desired outcome).
3) Interconnectedness: represents the affective-contextual dimension of hope—recognition of the interdependence and interconnectedness between self and others and between self and spirit (Herth, 1991; Herth, 1992).

Translating these social science concepts into more common language, one can say that three important parts of hope are the participant's perception or belief that a positive outcome is possible, that there is some confidence in being able to achieve this, and that through working with others (and at times drawing on spiritual resources) this will be possible.

How can workers make hope real for the people they serve? The previous section on dignity spoke to the importance of treating participants as valuable and worthy people who can accomplish much. Self-determination is an important factor. In stressing that people can choose for themselves, participants can realize that careful choices and hard work can lead to a better future. The strengths perspective, which will be discussed next, can help participants understand their capabilities and possibilities. There are also other things that can foster hope.

Giving people the opportunity to think about how things could be better in the near future can be useful. Chapter 10 provides a planning

*The Pathway of Hope, adopted in 2012, is an approach of Salvation Army social services to provide targeted services to families desiring to break the cycle of crisis and enable a path out of intergenerational poverty. The approach will be discussed in later chapters.

tool for doing some "realistic dreaming," which can then become the basis for actions.

Staff can enhance a person's sense of hope by giving that person information about available resources in the community. A participant working as a nurse's aide states that she would like to become a Licensed Practical Nurse. She knows she could do the work. However, she never could afford the tuition, even if she were a part-time student. Letting the woman know about scholarships, grants, and the possibility of subsidized child care may open up a window she had viewed as closed.

Workers can fan the flames of hope by helping people accomplish small goals, and then use that experience of success to move on to larger goals that fit into their vision of a better future. When people don't believe their efforts will pay off, they often cannot generate enough energy or persistence to see a task through. The sense of being able to realize one's dreams comes from experiences of being successful. Even small successes help. When workers help participants develop a sense of themselves as competent people, the participants will dream bigger and work to convert those dreams into reality.

Workers can listen carefully to the dreams of participants and help them work towards reaching them, even if the goal as first stated is not possible. Dennis Saleebey (1997) shares the story of a man with a diagnosis of chronic undifferentiated schizophrenia who told his social worker he wanted to be a pilot. Together they began to work towards that future. After some exploration of possibilities, the man was able to find a job as a dishwasher and then as a busboy at an airport restaurant, although the work involved an hour-long bus ride each way. At the time of the writing, he had gotten to know workers at the airport, who were helping him attain a job as a baggage handler, which paid well, with good benefits. It would have been easy to dismiss this individual's dreams as a delusion; instead, the worker helped nurture those dreams and move the participant towards a better future.

Believing in participants' abilities to attain their goals is essential. When people are dispirited, often workers need to believe in them first before they can believe in themselves. This is the social nature of hope. Whether in a church community, in a support group, or with a few friends, it is easier to have hope in the future when hope is shared by others.

A woman who with her family had

been homeless, and had stayed at The Salvation Army's Evangeline Booth Lodge in Chicago, expressed how workers there had supported them and instilled a sense of hope for the future:

> My husband Wardell says, "The Lodge opened doors for me that I could not otherwise have entered. After coming here, I went into the hospital. While I was in the hospital, the staff at the lodge treated my family with the utmost respect and were patient with me during the recovery period. The ultimate blessing came as I was working at a very low-paying job, and they helped me find a new job to support my family." Our stay at the Lodge has taught me many things. Among them is the fact that life is like a circle. As a popular song says, this circle moves all through hope and despair, through faith and love. As we prepare to move into a new home, I'm sure that we and others like us will rejoin this circle of life determined to stay (Ryan-Bailey, 1996).

Hope embedded in religious belief is a reality for many people. The story in Exodus about wandering in the wilderness and finally being able to reach the Promised Land is one that resonates with many people.

Workers need to help individuals discover there can be hope in their lives. Workers can also combat those situations in society where hopelessness is institutionalized. When half the students drop out of a high school, it is clear many do not see education as a road to a better future. Concerned helpers need to speak out. When depression and substance abuse rates are high in a community, it is clear many people see no hope for the future. Concerned helpers need to speak out.

Jim Wallis (1994) wrote that we live in a time when people are asked to accept the current political and economic situation as the way things always will be. To believe otherwise is considered nonsense, but that kind of nonsense can lead to changes in thinking and ultimately to changes in society. He noted: "The nonsense of slave songs in Egypt and Mississippi became the hope that the oppressed would go free. The nonsense of a bus boycott in Montgomery, Alabama, became the hope that transformed a nation"(Wallis, 1994, p. 238). Hope, then, becomes the door from one reality to another—believing in spite of the evidence, acting on the beliefs, and watching the situation change (Locke, Garrison, and Winship, 1998).

Strengths perspective

What do you see when you look at this picture? Do you see a vase, or do you see two figures? Can you

Figure 3.2

switch between the two?

As humans, and as people working in social services, we are used to looking at those who come in for services in terms of their problems and needs—lack of food, lack of money, concerns about getting evicted, etc. This is a deficit perspective, and it is incomplete. We need to be able to switch from a deficit to a strengths perspective, looking for strengths and resources. Using the example of the picture above, we need to see both—to focus on the positives in the lives of those seeking our help more than on their needs and the negatives in their lives.

Dennis Saleebey, the social work educator largely responsible for the social work profession's emphasis on strengths, gives this definition: "Mobilize participants' strengths (talents, knowledge, capacities, resources) in the service of achieving their goals and visions, and the participants will have a better quality of life on their terms" (Saleebey, 1997, p. 1).

Unlike traditional case management programs, strengths-based case management activities focus on discovering participants' personal strengths and resources and empowering them to create their own solutions to the challenges they face (Hall, et al., 2002). This perspective is based on the concept that all people have worth, that they hold untapped possibility for growth—mentally, physically, emotionally, socially, and spiritually (Weick, *et al.,* 1989).

The emphasis on strengths is relatively recent, and one can ask: "Why did it take so long for social work and the human services to embrace the concept of basing the work with participants on strengths as well as on problems?" There are a number of reasons why the strengths perspective has not been commonly used.

The emphasis on individual shortcomings in understanding personal crises and dilemmas fits in well with the predominant American value of independence, the idea of "pulling yourselves up by your bootstraps." Imbedded in American culture is the idea anyone can become rich; therefore, if someone is struggling, the tendency is to look inward for the source of the "problem."

The emphasis on deficits and problems is also rooted in the history of social work, which emerged as a profession in the late nineteenth and early twentieth centuries. Any new profession is shaped by the major ideas of the time, and two major influences on the emergence of social work were the scientific method and Sigmund Freud.

The concepts of rationality and efficiency were seen as not only important for factories being expanded as the United States became more industrialized in the late 1880s, but applicable to other aspects of society as well. The term "scientific charity," which was used for the beginning of social casework at that time, made social work seem more "professional" (Trattner, 1998). To employ the scientific method, one begins with problem identification, then assessing and treating this problem; the focus on problems as the starting point has endured.

Sigmund Freud had a great influence not only on the development of psychiatry, psychology, and therapy but also on social work and the way casework has been practiced in this century. Freud's focus on the interior lives of his patients and their childhood history moved social work and social casework in this direction (Lubove, 1965). Freud's own background also was important in the development of his thinking:

> The historical accident that made Freud a physician who thought in medical metaphors has cast a long shadow. He tried to fit the discoveries that he was making about people's emotional makeup into the mechanistic medical model in which he had been trained. Since physical pathology always had substrata of dysfunctional organs or cells, he made the same assumption about psychopathology. Each layer of emotional sickness was thought to rest on a deeper layer, and the investigation of these deeper layers was thought to be appropriate treatment. The deeper one went, the better; the more attention one paid to the psychopathology, the closer one was to the deepest layer of disease, and the greater the chance for a cure (Waters and Lawrence, 1993, p. 57).

These are more than interesting historical facts. When workers interview applicants or participants, they often are looking for a cause of the participants' predicaments or issues. When they find one—substance abuse issues or family background—they can feel good at having figured out the problem's cause and begin to work on "fixing" that problem.

In reality, knowing one aspect of a person's situation does not tell the worker everything about a person, and the emphasis on a diagnosis or label may have undesirable results. A person struggling with schizophrenia becomes seen only as a schizophrenic. When that label is applied, other aspects of the person's character, experiences, background, and aspirations fade into the background (Saleebey, 1997). Workers need to be continually reminded that people are more than their "identified problem." A woman may be a survivor of domestic abuse, but she is more than that.

There are other reasons for the emphasis on problems. Many programs set up by governments as well as by nonprofit organizations are categorical programs, those that have certain criteria applicants must meet to receive the benefits or services. Supplemental Nutrition Assistance Program (SNAP, formerly Food Stamps) and free school lunches are examples of categorical programs, those in which the applicants' eligibility is based on how few resources they have. Another example is applying for Supplemental Security Income (SSI) because of a disability. Applicants have to prove (often time and time again) how disabled they are in order to get benefits.

Potential participants understand this. When people apply for benefits or services, they often present their situation in the most negative way possible, thinking that if they talk at all about potential resources, they will not be deemed deserving enough.

Also, many individuals are not used to talking about their lives in positive terms. As Saleebey points out, "One of the characteristics of being oppressed is having one's stories buried under the forces of ignorance and stereotype" (Saleebey, 1996, p. 301). In some households children and adolescents are far more encouraged than others to "dream big" and act on those dreams. Also, in some families more than in others the successes and strengths of the children as they are growing up are acknowledged and praised.When a participant comes in for help, it's easy to assume they have always been in crisis. Workers need to remember that "people have survived to this point—certainly not without pain and struggle—through employing their will, their vision, their skills and, as they have grappled with life, what they have learned about themselves and their world" (Saleebey, 1997, p. 49).

The generally accepted view is that people do not change much over time. However, in reality most of us function better at some points in our lives than at others. It may be that in other contexts and in other times a participant was functioning much better than is apparent at the moment he or she is seeking help. When workers ask about these other times participants were more successful, they gain another perspective on the person's situation (Locke, Garrison, and Winship, 1998).

There are a number of strengths and resources all people have. These include their personal qualities and skills. Individuals have skills that may have value in the world of work (such as the ability to run complicated machines in factories), skills that may be useful in daily living (such as auto repair), or in other aspects of life (such as playing music).

People also possess coping skills and knowledge. An example is a man who has been battling alcohol addiction for years, staying sober for months or even years at a time before relapsing. He has learned how to stay sober for long periods, even if he does not always apply his knowledge. There are also skills and attitudes individuals have developed that help them live on the streets.

One can think of strengths in three levels of abstraction or concreteness. The most tangible resources are the things one has, such as money or a car. Less concrete but very useful are the skills described in the preceding paragraph. Still less concrete but very real to individuals are their beliefs, rituals, stories, and customs.

The strengths perspective engages in practices that seek to empower the individual, family, or community. By determining goals and identifying resources, participants improve their situation within the context of full membership within their community. That is, they are accepted by and feel comfortable with others who live in the same area or share similar characteristics. Opening the door to membership means all are welcomed, valued, have dignity, have worth, and have something to contribute to make the whole better. Central to the strengths perspective is the notion that individuals desire to belong and to be recognized by others. When one is severed from the larger group, alienation, marginalization, and oppression can take root.

Ethical behavior—applying the Code of Ethics

The Salvation Army's Social Services Code of Ethics (Appendix A) has standards related to responsibility to participants, to colleagues, to society, and as professionals.

Confidentiality

The Army's National Social Services Standards Manual (second edition, December 2013) has the following standards related to Confidentiality/ Release of Information:

4.9.1 The program abides by the policies and procedures listed in *The Salvation Army Guidelines on Confidentiality and Protection of Personal Privacy* (Appendix B).

4.9.2 Information is released by the staff members without permission only when there is a perceived danger that withholding the information would put the life and/or safety of the participant or others at risk.

4.9.3 The program has a formal release of information form.

4.9.4 The program provides a copy of the signed release of information form to the program participant and keeps a copy of the release in the case record.

4.9.5 The staff do not talk about program participant information in public or open areas where program participants, visitors or other staff members are present.

4.9.6 The staff do not share information about one program participant with another program participant.

4.9. 7 The staff do not share inappropriate personal information with program participants.

The Salvation Army Guidelines on Confidentiality and Protection of Personal Privacy (Appendix B) provide detailed instructions on what to do if staff is asked to release information without participants' permission. This much relates to the statement at the beginning of this chapter about the way ethics and laws are related; there are Salvation Army policies stating what to do within the structure of existing laws.

In the area of confidentiality, Standards 4.9.5 and 4.9.6 relate to disclosing information about participants. These refer explicitly to situations in which information is disclosed in public spaces or with participants. But a more inclusive guideline would be that participants are only discussed with supervisors or in team meetings when that discussion is in the context of plans or concerns for that participant (not: "You'll never believe what Robert told me about his brother today!").

Also, participants are NEVER to be discussed in any identifiable way with anyone not directly working with participants. This means that unless there is a signed release of information and a clear reason for the conversation, workers do not discuss participants with workers at other organizations. Furthermore, participants are not to be discussed with family and friends in anything more than the most general terms. A worker can say, "A woman really unloaded on me today—such language!" But he or she would not provide ANY identifiable description of the woman.

Workers and officers also need to be aware of the layout of waiting rooms and other office workspaces and work to increase the confidentiality of conversations. In some places, reconfiguring of space utilization, room dividers, and white noise machines have aided in maintaining confidentiality.

Dual relationships and maintaining boundaries

According to The National Association of Social Workers, "Dual or multiple relationships occur when a professional assumes two or more roles at the same time or sequentially with a participant, including the blending of professional and nonprofessional relationships" (NASW, 2012). Several decades ago, the social work profession almost adopted a policy against any dual relationships, until practitioner's pointed out the realities for those who work in small towns and rural areas. The person who fixes a worker's car may be a former participant, and as former participants are welcomed onto boards and advisory committees, one has interactions with them. Additionally, one's fifth-grade daughter may be in the same class as a participant or former participant, and the worker and participant run into each other because of this.

There is a distinction between *boundary crossings* and *boundary violations.* A boundary crossing occurs when a worker is involved in a dual relationship with a participant or former participant that is not intentionally exploitive, manipulative, deceptive, or coercive. Boundary crossings are not necessarily unethical.

Boundary violations are conflicts of interest that harm participants or colleagues. These include:

1) Intimate relationships—physical sexual contact or a sexual relationship.
2) Personal benefit—the participant providing services for the worker (such as housecleaning).
3) Altruistic actions—giving gifts or services not available to other participants.
4) Purposefully socializing with participants.

Another form of dual relationships is *sequential relationships.* Individuals' lives change, and at times someone who has been a participant becomes employed by The Salvation Army or another organization. This is especially the case in the addictions field. Privacy and confidentiality come into play in not acknowledging publicly the former worker-participant role, such as mentioning in a group, "Jennifer, I remember when you were struggling with alcohol and pills."

The Salvation Army has additional complexities because participants may be Salvationists or corps members and may also volunteer in some capacity. In all these cases, it is essential to be mindful of the role one has at the time. One should not share information that pertains to an earlier role or relationship, especially when the person was a participant. When one sees a participant or a member of a participant's family in another context, be sure to keep roles and boundaries clear. For example, if a child is in an after-school program and the family receives food assistance, one would not make any reference of this to the child or to anyone in the after-school program.

In a dual relationship situation, Standard 4.9.7 becomes essential: "The staff do not share inappropriate personal information with program participants." Workers should be cautioned to take a very broad definition of "inappropriate" and to reflect on the purpose of any sharing of personal information. At times self-disclosure can be purposeful in working with a participant, but in cases of dual relationships, such sharing can be seen as an indication of friendship.

In this era of social media, it becomes even more difficult than before to be careful about what information is available to participants, potential participants, and others. If a worker uses Facebook, supervisors should not only monitor what the worker posts but also watch to make sure workers are not "tagged" in photos that could be embarrassing. Some people want to have a Facebook account to share photos and information with families and friends, but do not want participants to see anything of their personal lives. One option is to cancel one's current Facebook account and start another with a name not searchable. An example is someone named Nora Jane Miller, who informed her Facebook friends that if they wanted to stay in touch, they should look on Facebook for Enjay Emm (her initials spelled out).

In any situation where one is not sure if there is a boundary or dual relationship issue, seek the guidance of a supervisor.

Conclusion

By being aware of ethics and boundaries, values, and legal issues, we become more effective.

The ecologist Barry Commoner once wrote: "Everything is connected to everything else" (1971, p. 33), and this is very true of social services work. In this chapter, ethics and boundaries, values and the importance of legal issues have been discussed. Just as the lives of the participants we work with are complicated, so are the connections between the topics covered in this chapter. In becoming more aware of how each of these affects our work, we become more effective.

Reflection questions

1) What do you do to treat participants with dignity, as individuals who are more than the sum of their problems or circumstances?

2) When has it been difficult to respect the self-determination of a participant, given the choices they had made or were intending to make? What did you do in this situation?

3) On page 33 are the Salvation Army standards related to Confidentiality/Release of Information. For which of these standards does your corps/program perform well, and where is there room for improvement?

PART II

Theories and Practice

CHAPTER 4

Understanding Poverty

In Salvation Army social services, we work with many people who are "poor." Understanding the definitions and dimensions of poverty and the factors that impact people being poor helps us in our work.

Defining poverty

How does one define poverty? The United States government defines poverty using a set of money income thresholds based on family size. Only benefits in the form of money (wages, child support, unemployment assistance, Supplemental Security Income, etc.) are counted, not noncash benefits such as SNAP (Supplemental Nutrition Assistance Program, formerly Food Stamps). If a family's total income is less than the threshold for a family's size, then that family and every individual in it is considered in poverty. These guidelines are the same for the 48 contiguous states and do not take into account differences in housing prices or heating costs from one part of the country to another. Every year, the guidelines are adjusted for inflation, using the Consumer Price Index.

Using federal poverty guidelines, the Great Recession in 2008 caused the percentage of Americans in poverty to increase from 12.5 percent in 2007 to 16 percent in 2012 and 2013. In 2014, 14 percent of Americans were considered poor.

2016 POVERTY GUIDELINES FOR THE 48 CONTIGUOUS STATES AND THE DISTRICT OF COLUMBIA	
PERSONS IN FAMILY /HOUSEHOLD	POVERTY GUIDELINE
1	$11,880
2	16,020
3	20,160
4	24,300
5	28,440
6	32,580
7	36,730
8	40,890
For families/households with more than 8 persons, add $4,160 for each additional person.	

Poverty Guidelines

Figure 4.1

An alternative way of determining the extent of poverty, the Supplemental Poverty Measure has been developed by the Census Bureau (Short, 2013). That measure takes into account geographical differences in housing costs and also counts the value of noncash programs such as housing assistance, SNAP, and tax credits, notably the Earned Income Tax Credit (EITC). Using this measure, the national poverty rate would be four percentage points lower, around 10 percent.

Regardless of the method used to calculate poverty, it is clear that a substantial number of Americans are poor. According to poverty researchers Sheldon Danziger and Christopher Wimer (2014), the major reason we have such a high rate of poverty is:

> The benefits of economic growth are no longer shared by almost all workers, as they were in the quarter century after the end of World War II. In recent decades, it has been difficult for many workers, especially those with no more than a high school degree, to earn enough to keep their families out of poverty. This economic trend represents a sharp break with the past. Inflation-adjusted median earnings of full-time year-round male workers grew 42 percent from 1960 to 1973. But, four decades later, median earnings were $49,398 in 2012, four percent lower than the inflation-adjusted 1973 value, $51,670. Men with no more than a high school degree fared even worse (p. 17).

Factors other than wage stagnation keep wages low. Although less than five percent of wage earners make the minimum wage, the rate at which the minimum wage is set affects the pay of many other low-income workers (U. S. Bureau of Labor Statistics, 2014). Supervisors at retail establishments often make only a dollar above the minimum wage paid to entry-level workers.

Comparing the value of earnings from several decades ago to today, one sees that some things, such as televisions and other electronics, are less expensive than they were previously. But the cost of child care has risen faster than the increase in wages (Lowery, 2014). Housing costs compared to wages are especially high. According to the National Low-Income Housing Coalition (2014):

> In the United States, the 2014 two-bedroom Housing Wage is $18.92. This national average is more than two-and-a-half times the federal minimum wage, and 52 percent higher than it was in 2000. In no state can a full-time minimum wage worker afford a one-bedroom or a two-bedroom rental unit at Fair Market Rent.

Although the value of low-wage earnings decreases when inflation is taken into account, the percentage of Americans making low and relatively low wages has increased. Almost 14 percent of workers in the United States make less than $10 an hour, and another 38 percent make from $10 to $20 an hour. The high end of that range is $41,600 annually, certainly not in poverty, but it is only 175 percent of the poverty guidelines for a family of four (Gedeon, 2014). A single mother with three children making $41,000 would qualify for Women, Infants, and Children (WIC) benefits.

Another indication of the increase in the number of low-income Americans comes from a report that 51 percent of children in public schools are eligible for free or reduced school lunches; families making up to 185 percent of the federal poverty line can receive reduced-price school lunches (Southern Education Foundation, 2015).

Determinants of poverty

When working with participants living in poverty, three things that need to be considered are the present economic and social context, the individual's past life experience, and how they see themselves in the present and in the future.

How well is the economy doing, especially in a specific city, town, or region? One professional who has worked in helping individuals find jobs for several decades remarked that in the late 1990s, when the economy was booming, she received a call from a local factory: "I need someone who is vertical." The demand for workers was so high that the requirements for entry-level positions were very low. In times with higher unemployment, it is much more difficult for people with few job skills or an episodic job history to get hired. Other factors in a local area that affect employment are the availability of public transportation and job training programs.

The social context, how individuals are treated in the community or in the larger area, needs to be understood. Although some believe we live in a post-racial world, in far too many communities there is discrimination based on one's race and ethnicity. Additionally, many employers have failed to hire qualified applicants with a disability because the employers made snap judgments based on the individual's disability and ability to perform the essential job functions with or without reasonable accommodations (Hyman, 2014).

In understanding adults who are struggling, it is important to recognize that experiences growing up have long-term impacts. Findings from the Adverse Childhood Experiences Study (which has been replicated with similar results) show that negative events or conditions in childhood profoundly affect emotional and physical health as well as behaviors and decision making later in life (Felitti, et al., 1998).

A questionnaire about adverse childhood experiences was completed by over 70 percent of 13,494 adults who had undergone a standardized medical evaluation at a large Health Maintenance Organization (HMO). This was not a group with serious medical or social problems, but a general representation of the U.S. population. Respondents were asked to indicate if in childhood they had experienced:

1) The loss of a parent, through divorce or death.
2) Psychological and/or physical abuse by the parents.
3) Sexual abuse by anyone.
4) Substance abuse in the family.
5) Mental illness in the family.
6) Domestic violence.
7) The imprisonment of a family member.

More than half the respondents stated they had had at least one of these experiences, and more than a quarter had three or more adverse experiences. Persons who had experienced four or more categories of childhood exposure, compared with those with no adverse experiences, were four to twelve times more likely to suffer from alcoholism, drug abuse, or depression and to have attempted suicide (Felitti, et al., 1998). Persons with four or more adverse experiences were more than twice as likely to have serious job problems as those with none (Larkin, Fellitti, and Anda, 2011).

Negative experiences in the past can influence one's ability to function well and deal with stress in the present, while positive experiences in the past can be sources of strengths in present difficulties. As described in Chapter 3, skills and abilities one has formed and demonstrated in the past and the experience of overcoming adversity can be resources to draw on in facing current issues and problems.

For young people moving into adulthood, the extent to which one has had positive experiences also can play a part in their workplace success. In a class discussing David Shipler's book *The Working Poor,* college students talked about work ethic and workplace skills developed in part-time and summer jobs. However, students who came from inner cities described having fewer of these opportunities than students from suburbs and small towns who had often gotten jobs through family connections or their social network (Winship, 2014).

Individuals who are white and grow up in middle-class environments are familiar with conversational styles and norms that prepare them to function well in the culture of many work organizations. If that is not one's background, learning how to adapt one's communication is essential. Journalist Te-Nehisi Coates (2010), who grew up on the "mean streets" of Baltimore, wrote about how important it is to be able to understand appropriate behavior and ways of communicating in a specific area and to be able to modify one's behavior, or "code switch," as needed:

> One can safely call not backing down from a fight an element of a kind of street culture. It's also an element which —once one leaves the streets —is a great impediment. "I ain't no punk" may shield you from neighborhood violence. But it cannot shield you from algebra when your teacher tries to correct. It cannot shield you from losing hours when your supervisor corrects your work.

Obviously, not only the past is important. Whether an individual views a current difficult situation as a temporary obstacle to be overcome or just the way things are can make a big difference in how he or she reacts and how much energy is invested in making things better. An example about how one's belief about what is possible has an impact comes from a worker in a transitional housing program. When the worker challenged a participant on not following through with agreed-upon action steps, the woman replied: "I'm a single parent with five children; what do you expect?" (Weinberg, 2014).

Conclusion

Understanding what impacts a participant's economic well-being helps us be more empathetic.

There is a tendency to look at how well a person is doing only in terms of the person's abilities and motivation. Using the language of social psychology, this is the Fundamental Attribution Error: the tendency to place undue emphasis on internal characteristics to explain someone else's behavior in a given situation, rather than considering external factors (Krull, 2001). When we look at our own behaviors and actions, we tend to acknowledge external factors that have an impact on what we are able to do. But we do this much less in considering other people's situations. Understanding factors that impact a participant's economic well-being can help us work with them in a more empathetic manner.

Reflection questions

1) On pages 42, 43 is information on Adverse Childhood Experiences, how negatives (child maltreatment, domestic abuse, substance abuse, etc.) during one's early years impact behavior as an adult. How does this information help you understand the situation of some participants?

2) What information from this chapter helps you better understand individuals who come to The Salvation Army requesting assistance?

CHAPTER 5

The Why, How, and When of Change

Why, how, and when do people change? The answers to these questions are important to those working in social services, as the participants we work with are often in bad situations. Many would like things to be different and better, but they have had difficulties in the past making changes that would improve their situations. In this chapter we will look at what theorists and authors have written about change and how these theories and concepts apply to our work.

Transtheoretical Model of Behavioral Change

The Transtheoretical Model of Behavioral Change was developed by James Prochaska and Carlo DiClemente, based on the Stages of Change Model they developed in working with those with addictions and through a review of 18 therapy systems and approaches.

The Stages of Change Model (Prochaska and DiClemente, 1982) is about when people change. This model pictures change as a number of stages that all require changes in attitude to make progress. Change is depicted as a cycle—as opposed to an all-or-nothing step. The authors contend it is quite normal for people to require several trips through the stages to make lasting change. So in this sense, reaching

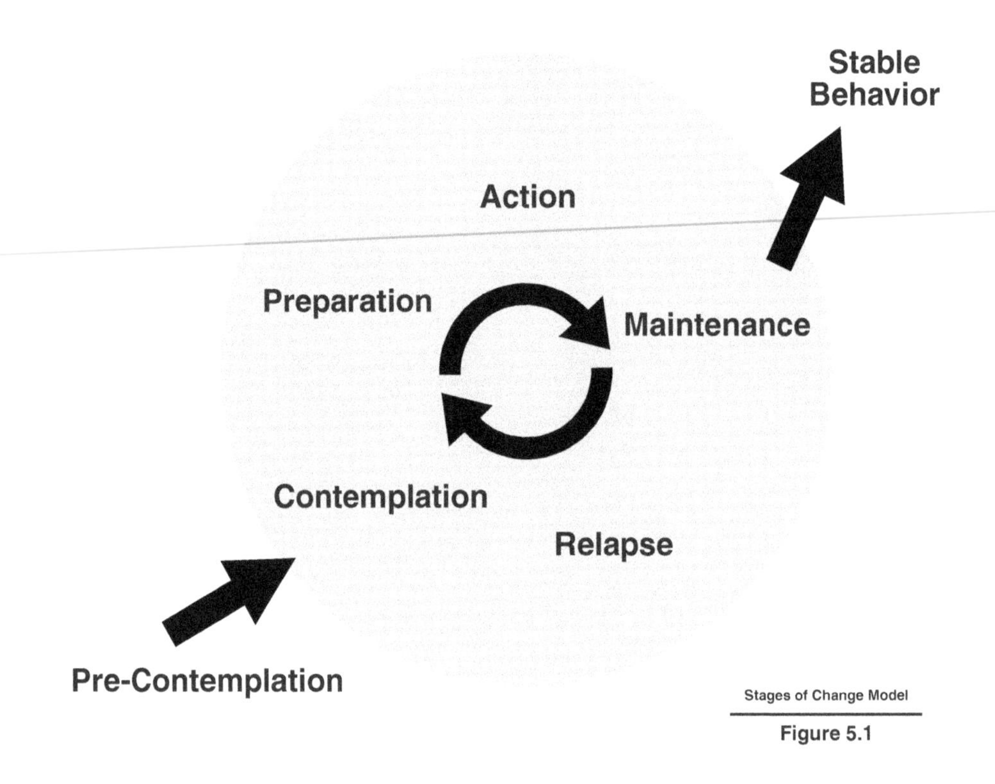

Stages of Change Model

Figure 5.1

goals and then slipping back is viewed as a normal part of the change process, as opposed to a complete failure. This does not mean this kind of relapse is desirable or even invariably expected. It simply means that change is difficult, and it is unreasonable to expect everyone to be able to modify a habit or way of doing things perfectly without any slips. The stages are:

Precontemplation Stage

This is not so much a stage of change as a prelude to formal stages. Persons could be said to be in Precontemplation when others see their behavior or habits as problematic and the persons are unconcerned about their situation. A smoker may be so busy with his work that his constant hacking cough doesn't distract him enough to consider it a significant problem. A heavy weekend drinker may not have any obligations on Sundays, so the fact he is throwing up most of Sunday morning isn't an immediate concern. It would be easy to call this "denial," but it would be more accurate to describe Precontemplation as a state when persons are "uninformed." In a sense, nothing yet has personally convinced them of the need for change.

Contemplation Stage

One can be said to be in the Contemplation Stage when one starts to think that maybe, perhaps, it might make sense to change. What frequently jars people into this stage, contemplating the possibility of change, is convincing, personal, and timely information—not coercion or even advice. People not yet contemplating change are not particularly open to advice, much less confrontation. We all have had the experience of someone telling us we must change some quality of ourselves. We are quite content, but others deem it unhealthy, unusual, or annoying. Information that makes a difference might come to a smoker in the form of a comment by his five-year-old daughter, "Please stop smoking, Daddy. I don't want you to die."

Preparation Stage

This is a transition period between shifting the balance in favor of change and getting things moving in that direction. Many people have fleeting moments of determination that vanish when they think of how big and how complicated the necessary changes in their life are. Preparation can lead directly into action when a person has the chance to thoroughly consider many aspects of the problem realistically, begin to make some changes and, at the same time, start to develop workable and effective goals.

Action Stage

It is truly remarkable what people are capable of once sufficiently motivated and invested in a realistic goal. The specifics depend on the issue or problem. However, it is essential for the person to work towards a goal or goals, not just work on a problem. With preparation, there is commitment both to making change and to realistic plans. In this process, taking small steps towards reaching goals can be reinforcing.

Maintenance Stage

Maintaining changes in behavior can be difficult. This applies equally to individuals attempting to live a less harmful lifestyle and to a single parent learning to live within a strict budget in order to keep her family housed. The advantage of labeling a stage "Maintenance" is that it highlights the work needed to hold on to gains that have been made.

Relapse

In the process of learning, of gaining experience in positive behaviors, slips occur. This is to be expected in some instances. It would be unreasonable to expect someone just starting to play the piano to be able to play Beethoven's *Moonlight*

Sonata perfectly after a month of lessons. Not being able to do so should not provoke such discouragement that the person gives up playing the piano (although some people certainly do). The same is true of addictive behavior or making other changes. Allowing the possibility of a slip will take some of the pressure and self-loathing away from the change process. Some people may need to go through the stages several times before lasting change occurs. Slips and setbacks are a part of learning. It is often through our mistakes that we learn where we need to put more effort in the future.

The Transtheoretical Model can be adapted to case management and other social services work. One valuable insight from this model is that the role of the worker can change, depending on what stage the participant is in. When the participant is in Precontemplation, the role may be that of a *nurturing parent,* akin to what a mother or father might do with a teen who is both attracted to and afraid of becoming more independent. With participants in Contemplation, the worker's role is like a *Socratic teacher,* who encourages the individuals to better understand their life and situation. With participants in the Preparation Stage, the role is more that of a *coach,* who can help the participants with a plan and (to use the coach analogy) with training. As participants implement the plan in the Action Stage, the worker's role can be more of a *consultant* in reviewing progress and helping the participant make adjustments (Norcross, Krebs, and Prochaska, 2011).

Motivational Interviewing

William Miller and Stephen Rollnick, who developed Motivational Interviewing from their experience with problem drinkers, define this approach as: "a collaborative conversation style for strengthening a person's own motivation and commitment to change" (2013, p. 12). The basis for Motivational Interviewing is that we all are ambivalent about the prospect of changes in our life and that arguments for and against change already reside within the ambivalent person. The worker's role is to intentionally guide a conversation so that the participant will explore and resolve the ambivalence. As this happens, motivation for change will increase.

Aspects of Motivational Interviewing are integrated throughout the following chapters of this book. These five questions for participants should give the reader a feeling of the Motivational Interviewing approach and its person-centered approach and style:

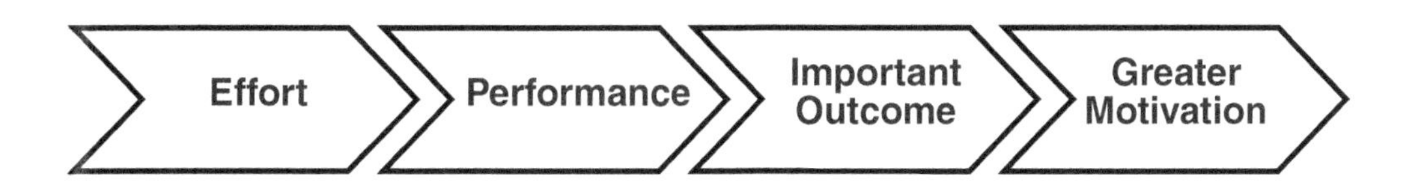

Importance Visualization

Figure 5.2

1) Why would you want to make this change?
2) How might you go about it in order to succeed?
3) What are the three best reasons for you to do this?
4) How important is it for you to make this change?
5) So what do you think you'll do? (Miller and Rolnick, 2013, p.11)

Expectancy Theory

The Expectancy Theory of Motivation, developed by Victor Vroom at Yale School of Management, can be adapted for social services work.

When individuals are contemplating an action and thinking of how much time and energy to commit to it, often they will informally estimate the likelihood the Effort will lead to successful Performance, and they will be able to do what they set out to do. This relates to the concept of self-efficacy, the ability of a person to complete tasks and reach goals. One's sense of self-efficacy is context-specific. A person may have a great deal of confidence based in past experience—for example, in being able to cook a deep-dish strawberry-rhubarb pie, but little self-efficacy when faced with speaking before a large group of people.

The second part of the Expectancy Theory is again an informal assessment. This assessment relates to the connection between Performance and the Importance of the outcome. If individuals believe they have the ability to carry out a plan AND completing it is important to them, they are more motivated to do what is necessary to turn the plan into reality. When either of the connections is weak, there will be less motivation (Vroom, 1965).

Reconciling the Rider and the Elephant

The images of the Rider and the Elephant come from the psychologist Joseph Haidt and have been popularized in Chip and Dan Heath's book Switch: *How to Change Things When Change Is Hard* (2010):

> Our emotional side is an Elephant and our rational side is its Rider. Perched atop the Elephant, the Rider holds the reins and seems to be the leader. But the Rider's control is precarious because the Rider is so small relative to the Elephant. Anytime the six-ton Elephant and the Rider disagree about which direction to go, the Rider is going to lose. He's completely overmatched (p. 7).

The Heaths maintain that our emotional and instinctive side, the Elephant, often opts for what would feel good now, instead of focusing on long-term gain. However, the Elephant also represents strong emotions, such as love, compassion, and loyalty. To be absorbed in doing something—that's the Elephant at work.

The Rider's strength is the ability to think long-term. But the weakness is that many of us tend to overanalyze things—to get so caught up in looking at the possible advantages and disadvantages of a decision that nothing gets done.

According to the Heaths, if a course of action has the Rider on board but not the Elephant, the participant will have understanding without motivation. If the decision is purely emotional, then there is passion without direction. The following approaches serve to engage both the Rider and the Elephant:

Finding the Bright Spots

"Bright Spots" refer to positive exceptions, times when things worked out better than they did most times. The authors use an example of a school counselor working with a fourth-grader who had learning disabilities and behavioral issues and was getting failing grades in almost all his classes. However, in one class he was doing well. When that teacher shared with other teachers her strategies for working with this student, the teachers were able to modify their approaches, and the student's performance in those classes improved.

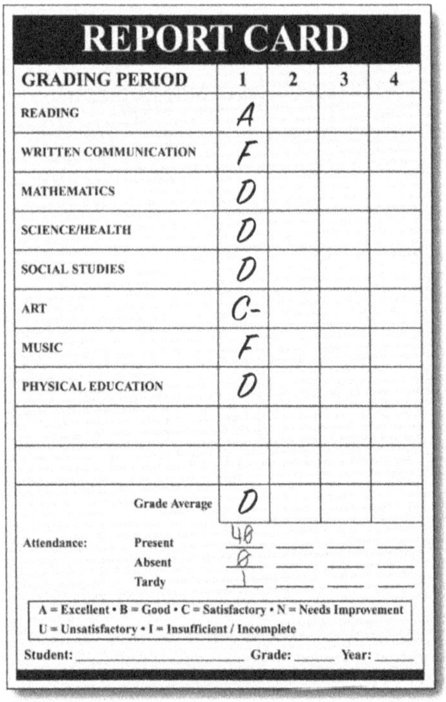

REPORT CARD

GRADING PERIOD	1	2	3	4
READING	A			
WRITTEN COMMUNICATION	F			
MATHEMATICS	D			
SCIENCE/HEALTH	D			
SOCIAL STUDIES	D			
ART	C-			
MUSIC	F			
PHYSICAL EDUCATION	D			
Grade Average	D			
Attendance: Present	48			
Absent	8			
Tardy	1			

A = Excellent • B = Good • C = Satisfactory • N = Needs Improvement
U = Unsatisfactory • I = Insufficient / Incomplete

Student: ______ Grade: ______ Year: ______

Shrinking the Change

Figure 5.3

Shrinking the Change

When individuals find a goal- or change-effort intimidating, one strategy is to make sure initial efforts seem possible and are very likely to be successful. Personal finance expert Dave Ramsey advocates the use of the "Debt Snowball." The first step for someone with a lot of credit card, utility, or other non-mortgage debt is to list everything in order, from smallest to largest. Then the minimum payments are made on most of the debt, and every available dollar is directed to the smallest debt on the list. When that is paid off, individuals move to the next smallest. Although this strategy seems to be counterproductive in that the "smartest" thing to do would seem to be pay off the debt with the highest interest rate or that could incur a late fee, the debt snowball works. It engages the Elephant in scoring a victory every time a debt—even a small one—is paid off, and that alleviates the sense of powerlessness.

Smoothing the Path

"Smoothing the Path" refers to making one behavior relatively simple to perform, so that it takes little effort to follow through. One clear example from the world of commerce is Amazon's "One-Click" feature. A shopper who has already entered a credit card and a shipping address can make a purchase moments after thinking, "Maybe I need this." When consumers cut up a credit card, they make the path to impulse shopping less smooth. Going back to money issues—paying bills on time—an individual can put bills into an envelope in the order in which they need to be paid, then mark on a calendar the date to pay them. The process can become routine.

Pointing to the Destination

The Rider needs a clear sense of the path to follow, and the Elephant, our emotional side, needs to be excited or energized about what life would be like if the goal or goals were reached. The Heaths use the concept of "postcard from the future" or destination postcards to describe the process of verbally drawing a vivid picture of the near future—of what life would be like after the hard work leads to goal completion.

A Better Future

Figure 5.4

In working with a family episodically homeless and very mobile, the parent could be asked to think about what it would be like for her children to be going back to the same school for a second or third year. How would that kind of stability benefit her children?

Conclusion

Applying these models/ideas of change are important to our learning.

The ideas and concepts presented here will be integrated into following chapters. It is important to be aware of *why* people change. The Expectancy Theory of Motivation helps us understand the importance of seeing the change as possible, and Chip and Dan Heath's technique of Pointing to the Destination shows that the possibility of a better future can engender or increase motivation to act. From Motivational Interviewing comes the idea that individuals are motivated when they work through conversations with a helper to resolve their ambivalence to change.

Motivational Interviewing also provides tools and techniques relevant to *how* people change. Some approaches from the Heaths, such as building on Bright Spots, are consistent with the Strengths Perspective and are valuable in change efforts. Matching the role of the worker to the participant's Stage of Change is essential, according to the Transtheoretical Theory of Change.

The Transtheoretical Theory of Change also provides us a way to look at the *when* of change and a lens to see where individuals are in relation to readiness to commit energy and resources to a change effort. This change is not a linear process—relapse is a normal part of it.

Reflection questions

1) How can you use the Stages of Change Model in your work?

2) According to the Expectancy Theory of Motivation (page 49), if individuals believe they have the ability to carry out a plan AND the result of having completed this is important, then they are more motivated to do what is necessary to turn the plan into reality. How can you use this in your work?

3) From the work of Chip and Dan Heath come the ideas of Finding the Bright Spots, Shrinking the Change, Smoothing the Path, and Pointing to the Destination (pages 50, 51). How can at least one of these be useful to you in your work?

CHAPTER 6

Working Towards Cultural Competence

Without a measure of cultural competence one cannot be effective in working with individuals. When culture is ignored, families and individuals are at risk of not being understood, not getting the support they need or, worse yet, not receiving helpful assistance.

Cultural competence can be seen as "the ability of individuals and systems to respond respectfully and effectively to people of all cultures, classes, races, ethnic backgrounds, sexual orientations, and faiths or religions in a manner that recognizes, affirms, and values the worth of individuals, families, tribes, and communities and protects and preserves the dignity of each" (Brohl, n.d.).

In *The Salvation Army Social Services Standards Manual* (2013), cultural competence is defined as "a set of attitudes and skills that enable the provision of service in a manner that is sensitive, respectful, and responsive to the differing backgrounds, customs, languages, values, expectations, etc., of those we serve. It means identifying ways of opening the door and becoming inclusive of people who might otherwise feel uncomfortable with us, or even excluded because of their differences. It calls us to go beyond statements of nondiscrimination to being proactive in bridging to others" (4.10).

The fifth principle in The Salvation

Army Social Services Code of Ethics (Appendix A) is: "Strive to understand culture and how this impacts human behavior and society, being sensitive to diversity and differences in people in the development of programs and case plans for various constituencies. Staff will avoid any derogatory language or any actions that could be interpreted as harassment." This statement includes three important aspects of cultural competence: sensitivity and understanding of the role of culture in human life; ability to apply that understanding to program design and individual interactions with those different from us; and avoiding bias and discrimination.

This chapter will look at how culture is defined, trace the continuum from cultural destructiveness to cultural awareness, describe the five steps of cultural competence, and apply our understanding to social services.

Definitions of culture

The term "culture" is most often used in reference to lifestyle or values of a group of people. We regularly associate culture with race and ethnicity, but as the first definition of cultural competence shows, culture encompasses much more than that. Individuals are composites of many factors, each with its own culture, such as nationality, language, spiritual tradition, profession, generation, and sexual orientation. This ties into the concept of social identities, discussed later in this chapter.

Culture can be understood as a way of life of a group of people or society, consisting of acceptable and accepted behaviors, beliefs, values, and traditions. It also can be defined as a set of meanings or understandings shared by a group of people—a framework, a worldview, or a cognitive map—that is used to make sense of the world. If we have not had extensive experience with others from differing backgrounds and cultures, we might assume the way we do things is the way everybody acts, and we view their behavior through our cultural worldview.

One way to think of culture is through the concept of an iceberg. If one is approaching an iceberg in a ship, one can see a mountain of ice, but there is much more of the iceberg below the surface. Similarly, from the vantage point outside a particular culture, one notices certain aspects of a culture, such as language, way of speaking, dress, typical foods, etc. Yet primarily out of one's awareness are other beliefs, attitudes, and patterns of behavior that also are significant. These can include body language, ideals governing child raising, roles within a family, norms around social interaction with friends, acquaintances, and strangers, and much, much more.

Sociologist Ann Swidler's (1986) perspective is also useful. She suggests that culture should be thought of as a "tool kit of symbols, stories, rituals, and worldviews" that we acquire as we grow up in particular social environments. These are more like skills or preferences than values. From childhood into adulthood, we are exposed to and acquire ways of speaking, including a language or languages and a vocabulary.

We learn how to relate to a group or groups of people, and we may be taught or acquire certain skills. Depending on the household and social environment, these skills might include auto repair, farming, cooking, computer graphics, or surveillance for the possible arrival of police. Depending on our situation as adults, the skills we developed earlier in our lives may or may not be useful at that point in time.

The concept of culture can also be applied to the professional and bureaucratic environments our participants encounter. Participants enter a shelter or social services organization requesting specific help. They find themselves in an environment in which the words and acronyms used are often unfamiliar, where the participants are asked to perform certain tasks or follow rules that may not make sense to them.

Additionally, there are wide disparities in the ways participants are viewed in organizations serving those in need. A participant with experience in navigating one social services agency may feel lost in another organization where not only policies are different, but it is not clear what is appropriate behavior.

Clearly, culture overlaps race and ethnicity. This may be especially apparent in the case of recent immigrants, whose upbringing in their country of origin forms the basis for their understanding of events and customs. Also, for many immigrants, living in the United States is the first time they have experienced prejudice and oppression.

Cultural sensitivity and cultural competence

Cultural sensitivity or cultural awareness is not the same as cultural competence. Cultural awareness can be thought of as being sensitive to diversity and having some level of understanding of people who look, think, and/or behave differently than us. Cultural competence goes beyond that to having the ability to work effectively across differences. If one considers cultural competence to be a continuum, then one can think of related attitudes and beliefs as ranging from cultural destructiveness to cultural competence (adapted from the National Center on Cultural Competence, n.d.).

Cultural destructiveness

The term "cultural destructiveness" refers to policies, structures, attitudes, and practices within organizations that are destructive to a cultural group. An example of this is the American Indian boarding schools of the late nineteenth and early twentieth centuries that banned students from speaking their native language or having any interactions with their family or home community. By the time these students returned to their communities, they no longer were able to communicate with their parents or understand their culture.

Cultural incapacity

This refers to attitudes and policies that value or privilege one's own culture and behaviors over others. Differences are acknowledged, but usually devalued, often through the use of stereotypes. Blaming some cultural difference for the economic status of a disadvantaged group is an example of cultural incapacity. An example of this comes from William Ryan's classic book *Blaming the Victim* (1971). In blaming the victim, we identify some current social condition, such as poverty, that is more prevalent in some ethnic minority groups than in the general society. Then we identify some aspects of their culture—beliefs, values, customs, or behaviors—that are distinct from that of the white majority. The poverty is then blamed on individual/cultural factors, ignoring any social or economic factors.

Cultural blindness

This is the expressed philosophy and practice of treating everyone the same, in essence saying that one's race, ethnicity, gender, sexual orientation, and/or disability status are inconsequential. When someone says, "I don't see color," what is behind that statement may be a well-intentioned statement about not being prejudiced. However, with cultural blindness, one is ignoring important parts of an individual's identity.

Cultural awareness and pre-competence

In this stage is a level of awareness of the important role that culture plays in beliefs, outlook, and actions. The individual worker is developing an appreciation of diversity and a commitment to human and civil rights. However, there are large gaps in knowledge and skills in being able to effectively work with people who look, think, and/or behave differently from oneself. This stage in some ways is akin to the Contemplation Stage in the Transtheoretical Stages of Change Model. The worker is conscious or cognizant that much more work needs to be done to be effective within differing cultural contexts.

Moving towards achieving cultural competence

The term "moving (or working) towards achieving cultural competence" is used because stating that a person is culturally competent implies the person has reached the desired level of knowledge or skill. In reality, as cultures and situations are always changing, workers need to be in a continuous process of learning, with an attitude of cultural humility—a commitment to ongoing learning and understanding (Morgaine and Capous-Desyllas, 2015).

Steps towards cultural competence

One approach to being in the process of working towards cultural competence, building on the work of Terry Cross, *et al.* (1989), involves five steps:

1) Acknowledging cultural differences.
2) Understanding one's own identities and culture.
3) Engaging in self-assessment.
4) Viewing behavior within a cultural context.
5) Acquiring cultural knowledge and skills.

The first step of acknowledging cultural differences involves moving past the stage of Cultural Blindness. It is common for workers, who for the first time work with individuals whose background and racial/ethnic identity are different from their own, to minimize the differences between themselves and their participants. If the worker is a parent, in conversations it may become apparent that both worker and participant share similar issues in child raising. There is also a tendency to focus on those parts of the human condition that are universal and pay less attention to other differences. Once one has acknowledged the reality of cultural differences (moving from Cultural Blindness), the next two steps—understanding your own identities and culture and engaging in self-assessment—can be done more or less at the same time.

In the simplest terms, one's identity is the answer to the question: "Who am I?" The answer is not simple, for all of us have more than one identity. In the language of the Social Identity

Theory, we define ourselves by the social categories we belong to—such as nationality/national origin, occupation, gender roles, family roles—and our identity is also influenced by the way these identities are viewed by society (Tajfel and Turner, 1986). In addition to this, we all have a personal identity based on our self-concept and self-knowledge. Examples of this personal identity would be "I am an introvert" and "I am a caring, compassionate person."

While it would be impossible to come up with a complete list of social categories or social identities, some common ones are:

1) Age (middle-aged, teenager, young adult).
2) Race (African-American).
3) Occupation (airline pilot, factory worker).
4) Ethnicity (German, Latino/Hispanic (more narrowly as Mexican), or Guatemalan).
5) Body type/characteristics (thin, obese, tall, short).
6) Religion (Christian, Muslim, Jew).
7) Urban/rural.
8) Family role (as sister, grandparent, living alone, mother of young children).
9) Sexual orientation.
10) Gender and gender identity—including transgender persons (see http://www.wikihow.com/Respect-a-Transgender-Person for tips on respecting transgender persons).

In Figure 6.1, Understanding Our Social Identities (next page), workers are asked to list identities they have within certain categories. In some cases a worker will use a ten-point scale to indicate how important this identity is to the worker, how apparent this identity is to someone who just met the worker, and how this identity is positively and/or negatively valued by society. We can gain an understanding of areas in which we do and do not have privilege and can compare these to the situation of the participants with whom we work.

Also, it is valuable to use this exercise in staff training to encourage staff members to discuss the importance of their personal identities. One advantage of such a discussion is that it is easy to assume which identity is most important for a given co-worker. For many people living in the U.S. whose ancestors came to this country many generations ago, their ethnicity may not be highly valued. For others, who are first- or second- generation Americans, or who come from close knit ethnic communities, that ethnic identity may be very important to their self-identity. For some individuals—and this cuts across boundaries of race, ethnicity, and social class—their spirituality or religious beliefs and practices may be the identity most important to them. For others, who rarely go to church, read the scriptures, or pray, their religious beliefs and practices are not a significant part of their identity.

Specify in each category how you identify yourself— ***For example, under "Gender": male or female***	How important is this identity to you?	How apparent is this identity to someone who only sees you or does not know you well?	How highly regarded is this identity by society as a whole? ***Explain reasons for positive valuation by society***	**Explain reasons for negative valuation by society**
	Scale: 1-10 (Ten is the highest score)			
Race:				
Ethnicity (where your ancestors or "people came from:				
Social class (middle class, working class, poverty):				
Gender and Gender identity:				
Sexual identity:				
Ability/Disability (able-bodied, with cerebral palsy, etc.):				
Spirituality/Religion, Membership in faith community:				
Occupation/Proposed occupation:				
Language Preference (English, Spanish, Hmong, etc):				
Membership in social organization:				
Other:				

Understanding Our Social Identities

Figure 6.1

Many things have helped shape our beliefs, values, and attitudes about children, families, men and women, and poverty and success. These include our family of origin, our upbringing, and the values and attitudes of others in the communities, areas, and nations in which we have lived. The following questions, adapted from an Annie E. Casey Foundation guide to cultural and linguistic competence (Hepburn, 2004), may be helpful. Answering them can make clearer the impact of the workers' upbringing and community on their attitudes and their knowledge of others who look, think, and/or behave differently than they do:

1) What social interaction with people from ethnic groups, socioeconomic classes, religion, age groups, or communities did the worker have when growing up?
2) Does the worker or anyone in his or her family speak a language other than English? If so, what language and how has it influenced the worker's interactions with others? If not, what was the predominant attitude in the worker's family about people living in the U.S. who spoke languages other than English?
3) What attitudes towards other cultural groups did the worker's family of origin have? How are the worker's attitudes similar or different?
4) What values, beliefs, or cultural messages* did the worker receive about education and learning from his or her family of origin and others the worker spent much time with growing up?
5) What values, beliefs, or cultural messages did the worker receive about success and the reasons people are successful from his or her family of origin and from others the worker spent much time with growing up?
6) What values, beliefs, or cultural messages did the worker receive about poverty and the reasons people are poor from his or her family of origin and from others the worker spent much time with growing up?
7) Has the worker ever felt uncomfortable, upset, or surprised by any expectations of his or her professional education, training, or orientation? If so, what was in question and what was the outcome?
8) Has the worker questioned his or

*Cultural messages are what everyone in a group knows that outsiders do not know. They come from family, neighbors, classmates at school, and others. Just as a fish does not know he is swimming in water, we are unaware of how many of our values, attitudes, and beliefs we absorbed without thinking about them.

her personal values, beliefs, and behaviors as a result of the worker's training/education (in school, workshops, webinars, etc.)? If so, what was in question and what was the outcome?

9) Does the worker ever find his or her personal beliefs and values in conflict with those of colleagues or others in the worker's organization? If so, how does the worker resolve it?

10) Does the worker ever find his or her personal beliefs and values in conflict with those to whom the worker provides services? If so, how does the worker resolve it?

11) What personal qualities does the worker have that will help establish interpersonal relationships with persons from other cultural and linguistic groups? What personal qualities might be detrimental?

Just as the steps of understanding one's identities and culture and of engaging in self-assessment can be worked on at the same time, so can the fourth and fifth steps of Terry Cross' model on achieving cultural competence (1989). In viewing behavior within a cultural context and acquiring cultural knowledge and skills, there is an ongoing interaction between learning and applying it to understanding and acting in new ways. Although the distinction between acquiring knowledge and developing skills is not always clear, the following paragraphs begin with acquiring knowledge and information, followed by skill application.

In our quest to become culturally competent, it is natural to want to find information that will explain the values, attitudes, and actions of groups with whom we are unfamiliar. One common approach is to say, "I am going to learn about a group, like Hispanics/Latinos*." This approach encourages broad generalizations of a group and can lead to forming stereotypes.

It has been common in social work education textbooks to include a chapter on ethnic minority groups, with a few pages on each group. In one of the most widely read social work practice textbooks (Kirst-Ashman and Hull, 2012), fatalism is said to be a characteristic of Native American and Latino cultures. Fatalism is the concept that events are predetermined and therefore inevitable—whatever will be, will be.

---

*One frequent question is, "What is the better term—Latinos or Hispanics?" There is no term generally agreed upon by those whose ethnicity originated in Latin America. Asking people how they want to be referred to is always a good idea. In many cases, people will prefer to be identified by their country of origin, as Mexicans or Brazilians, for example.

In adopting a fatalistic attitude towards life, one feels powerless to change one's situation in life.

To what degree does this apply to Hispanics and Native Americans/ First Nation individuals? The best answer: "It all depends." One factor that comes into play is the degree of cultural assimilation and acculturation into mainstream American culture. Cultural assimilation refers to one group assuming the values, practices, and language of a dominant group.

Many of us in the United States are the descendants of people who immigrated from Italy, Germany, or Scandinavian countries a century or more ago. For the most part, by the second or third generation, the native language was not spoken much around the house. Although the descendants may maintain certain foods and holidays, most of us whose descendants arrived here generations ago have largely assimilated into American society. However, some immigrants try to hold onto their native language and do not become largely assimilated into American culture.

Acculturation (or biculturalism) refers to a process whereby an immigrant or a person from an ethnic minority group acquires enough of the language, values, and common practices of the dominant culture to function effectively in it, without giving up the language and values of the country of origin. The degree of assimilation or acculturation can influence the degree to which fatalistic attitudes persist.

In the case of fatalism, understanding a person's prior life experience may be a stronger indicator of a fatalistic attitude than one's ethnicity. If one grew up in a family in which job loss and/or homelessness happened over and over again, or one's parents were never able to get ahead regardless of what they did, the person may adopt a fatalistic attitude. On the other hand, if the person and others close to him or her have been able to consistently overcome challenges in their life experiences, the person is much less likely to adopt a fatalistic attitude towards life.

One does not use general information about ethnic minority and other disadvantaged/oppressed groups to form conclusions in advance. However, in interactions with members of these groups, one can check the accuracy of the information in a particular situation. With this information on fatalism, for example, in conversation with participants one may be looking for indicators as to whether fatalism is or is not present. One can use information on groups different from one's own not to form judgments but to pay attention to certain behaviors. After reading that in some ethnic minority groups, the wife is subservient to the husband, a worker might be especially watching and listening for this in the interactions between husband and wife.

How best then to get the information workers need to move towards cultural competence? In many cases, one does not need to know about all ethnic minority or immigrant groups. But it is critical for workers to understand as much as possible about those they work with.

In the case of immigrants, there is a phenomenon called the "migrant trail." Individuals from one city, village, or area of a country will immigrate to another country, in this case the United States. Relatives and friends who also have decided to leave will join them in the communities where they have settled. This happened in the 1800s in the United States, when neighborhoods in Milwaukee were settled by immigrants from one German city and small towns in northern Minnesota were settled by Norwegians from a rural area in Norway. In one small city in Wisconsin, currently over 15 percent of the population is Latino. It turns out that a considerable number of them came from one rural area in the State of Guanajuato in Mexico.

Once the specific groups/communities have been identified, one very good approach is to use "cultural informants." These are members of that community who are acculturated or bicultural, understand the culture and customs of their home area, and know how to communicate this to someone outside that culture. If the workers have identified such a person, they can then ask questions such as: "A participant came in today and told me something I did not understand. Can I run this by you and get your take on what I am missing?"

Applying our understanding to social services practice

How one applies an increasing degree of cultural competence will vary greatly from program area to program area, based on which group one is working with. Below are several suggestions for becoming more effective:

1) *Serve as a "culture broker."* For new immigrants or those who have recently moved to the community, help the family identify and resolve value conflicts. For example, a person may feel pride about some aspects of his or her ethnic background and shame

about others, or may experience an immobilizing "tug of war" between personal aspirations and family loyalty.

2) *Be aware of "cultural camouflage."* Participants sometimes use ethnic, racial, or religious identity (and stereotypes about it) as a defense against change or pain or as a justification for halfhearted involvement in planned change efforts. A person who says "I'm late for a scheduled appointment session because I'm Puerto Rican" may be trying to avoid a difficult issue.

3) *Know there are advantages and disadvantages in being of the same ethnic group as your participant.* There may be a "natural" rapport because of belonging to the same "tribe" as your participant. Yet, a worker may also unconsciously over identify with them. Unresolved issues about the worker's ethnic identity may get in the way.

Conclusion

Cultural competence is a lifelong process.

As we develop greater awareness and abilities to work with specific groups of people whose life experience and culture differ from our own, we are likely to realize the approaches we use in working with them are applicable across a much broader range of people. In addition to using the reflection questions listed below and looking for resources in your home community, the corps also can request cultural competence training from their divisional multicultural ministries coordinators or social services directors.

As stated in the Army's *National Social Services Standards Manual:* "Cultural competence is not something easily or quickly achieved. It is a lifelong process that includes training, self-examination, and creative responsiveness to local needs and conditions." The following reflection questions and activities can help. Also, corps could contact their divisional multicultural ministries coordinators or social services director and request cultural competence training.

Reflection questions

1) In what ways is your facility (workplace) "opening the door" to ensure that people feel welcomed and included? How are you being proactive in bridging to others?

2) Thinking about the "concept of culture as an iceberg," how would you describe the culture of your workplace? What are the things you notice? What things are important and might not be visible (like the iceberg under the water) to persons unfamiliar with your workplace?

3) Where do you consider you are on the continuum of Cultural Competence (pages 58,59)?

4) Another activity that may help you explore "Identity" is at https://www.youtube.com/watch?v=lP_Ia0Zitdg. It is called "Who Am I?" with Eric Law. After viewing the video, take time to participate in the activity. This can also be used in a staff meeting or for staff training.

5) Complete the questions about cultural and linguistic competence on pages 62, 63. After answering these questions, what new insights did you gain about your culture?

CHAPTER 7

Skills and Techniques for Effective Practice

The skills and techniques presented here are connected to the chapters in Part III: Working with Individuals, Families and Communities. At times there will be elaboration of the areas which cover the following skills and techniques, or tools: nonverbal communication, use of questions, reflections, summarizations, affirmations, and self-disclosure. The last part of the chapter will highlight cautions or approaches to avoid because they are not effective.

Nonverbal communication

Workers need to pay attention both to their own and to participants' nonverbal communication. Nonverbal communication covers everything communicated except the meaning of the words spoken. Voice tone and volume are nonverbal cues. So are gestures, posture, eye movements, breathing patterns, physical appearance and, in the case of the worker, the arrangement of the office desk and chairs. Researchers state that in a conversation between two people, nearly two-thirds of the meaning each gets from that conversation is communicated nonverbally (Calero, 2005).

A worker can learn much by paying attention to a participant's nonverbal behaviors. Nonverbal cues can alert the worker to the participant's stress and comfort levels regarding the situation and the topic being discussed. For example, a participant who covers his mouth or puts his hands over his chest when a subject comes up may be communicating discomfort or pain related to the topic.

The worker also communicates to the participant through nonverbal behaviors. When workers are paying close attention to participants' words and are not distracted by the phone or other sounds, concern is communicated. On the other hand, a worker's clothing, gestures, loud voice, or fidgeting may communicate to the participant that this person is not interested or not competent.

It is very important that the worker display *congruence* (a fit between verbal and nonverbal behaviors). Workers saying they really want to be of assistance while constantly looking at their phone demonstrate a lack of congruence. When there is a lack of congruence, the participant is likely to believe the nonverbal message or become confused.

When "reading" and responding to an individual's emotions, it is important to remember that we rely on nonverbal communication for much of our meaning about what an individual is feeling. Also, the meaning of a nonverbal sign can change from one culture to another. If a worker is unsure of the meaning of the nonverbal communication of a participant from a race or culture different from his or her own, talking with a cultural informant* may be advisable (as stated in the previous chapter).

Use of questions

We ask participants questions because we need to understand their situation to see if they qualify for services, to see if we can be of help in other ways, to help them clarify their issues—and for a variety of other reasons. How we ask questions not only affects the information we receive but also impacts our relationship with the participant.

Closed questions significantly narrow a participant's range of responses by focusing on very specific information. Closed questions frequently begin with words such as "will," "is," "are," "did," "when," and "where."

They usually require a "yes" or "no" response or only a brief answer. Examples:

---

*Cultural informants are members of a community—racial/ethnic/sexual orientation, etc.—that are acculturated or bicultural, who understand the culture and customs of their community and know how to communicate this to someone outside it.

1) "Are your children living with you?"
2) "When will you start to receive disability benefits?"
3) How much is your rent?"

Closed questions can be useful for clarifying responses to questions. If a woman is describing the moves she has made since a divorce, and all three of her children were not with her all the time, the worker may use a closed question: "Was your older daughter staying with her grandparents then?"

An indirect closed question is a statement that implies a question but does not end with a question mark. An example of an indirect closed question would be: "I need your date of birth."

Closed questions are useful in getting specific information needed for paperwork. However, when workers ask a series of closed questions to obtain needed information, participants can feel interrogated and defensive to the point of anger. Whenever possible, it is advisable to ask open questions.

An open question is phrased in such a way that participants feel free to answer in as many or as few words as they choose. The following examples contrast open and closed questions. While the topic is the same, the responses will be very different:

1) Do you have a good relationship with your direct supervisor at your job?
2) What can you tell me about your relationship with your direct supervisor at your job?

With the first question, the participant may elaborate, or may just say,"It's okay." Then follow-up questions would be needed. The second example, an open question, invites details about how the participant gets along with the supervisor.

Open questions usually begin with words like "What," "How," or "Could" and encourage the participants to elaborate on the topic. The questions invite a two-way conversation and are key to encouraging participants to do most of the talking. The following are examples of open questions:

1) How can I help you with this issue?
2) What have you tried before when things were this difficult?
3) Could you tell me about your son's behavior since you had to go to the shelter?

Open-ended questions are generally more effective when they ask about specific experiences, behaviors, or feelings. When questions are too open, they can lead to broad, general, brief responses. If a worker were asked by a friend, "How's life," his or her initial reply might be something like, "Okay, I guess" or "Pretty good." When we use specific questions as the examples given above, we are much more likely to get the information we need to understand the situation.

As with closed questions, there are several kinds of indirect open questions. The use of "I statements" makes the request for information more personal. An example would be: "I've been wondering about how your daughter is doing in her new school." Most people would respond by recounting the daughter's experience. A second example of indirect open questions would be: "I'd like to hear more about how you managed to quit smoking." Still another indirect open question starts with the words "Tell me ... " An example would be, "Tell me what you've done to get a job."

Indirect questions can be productive in that they don't come across as interrogation and can communicate interest and concern on the part of the worker. Another way of softening questions is to qualify them, as in: "Would you care to tell me how this happened?"

A variation on open questions is called Questions for Solutions, part of the solution-focused approach developed by Steve de Shazer and Insoo Kim Berg (1994) and colleagues in the Brief Therapy Center in Milwaukee. Questions are used to permit participants to recount what they have tried, how they have coped in the past, when things in a problematic situation have been better, and what a difference in their lives would look like (DeJong and Berg, 1998). Examples of this are given in Chapter 9.

When properly posed, questions can be useful in gathering information and understanding a situation. However, some questions are by their nature inappropriate. These include:

Double questions—Asking two (or sometimes three) questions at the same time. Although the individual questions may be appropriate, participants tend to get confused and not know which to answer. Examples:

1) "Have you decided to stay at your old job or apply for a new one?"
2) "Can I help you with this problem, or would you rather wait?"

"Why" questions—When asked "Why," participants often try to

come up with the motivation or reasons behind a decision or action. Often, multiple factors are involved. Asking "Why" questions can stop an interview dead in its tracks or create defensiveness on the part of the participant. Instead of asking, "Why did you get so stressed out at your last job," the worker might ask: "What were some things that were stressful about your last job?"

Statement questions—These appear to be in the form of a question, but the worker is really stating his personal opinion. Such questions clearly express a worker's views on the situation or ideas about what the participant should do. Examples:

1) "Wouldn't it be better if we waited until next time?"
2) "How difficult is it to get your kids to bed at a decent hour?

Loaded questions—Similar to the statement question, loaded questions are direct questions about sensitive areas, asked in an accusatory way. Loaded questions may also make an assumption about facts or actions not necessarily true. The classic example of this, which assumes infidelity has occurred, is: "Are you still cheating on your wife?" Another type of loaded question seeks information and at the same time can come across as insulting to the participant. An example of this is: "Do you really think ignoring your landlord will solve the problem?"

Reflections

A reflection is a paraphrase or restatement of something the participant has said. When workers paraphrase the facts, opinions, and beliefs of a participant, they are *reflecting content*. After a participant has unleashed a torrent of words about his present troubles, touching on at least six different issues, the worker might use a reflection of content to clarify the worker's understanding: "So, you left the job after they only gave you hours on nights and weekends."

Workers *reflect feelings* by accurately identifying the emotional aspects of a participant's words and nonverbal behavior and then communicating the worker's perception of those feelings. Frequently, there will be a discrepancy between the words and the nonverbal behavior. Most often, nonverbal behavior is a more accurate indicator of true feelings. An example of a reflection of feelings could be: "You're really upset with your family."

Combined reflections include references to both the content and the emotions of a participant's verbal and nonverbal communication. This type of reflection can be very useful in demonstrating empathy. It shows the participant that the worker understands what he or she is feeling and why. The formula: "You feel __________ because __________" can be useful for making combined reflections, but it can sound stilted or forced, especially if repeated. As workers become more comfortable, they can become more spontaneous and natural in phrasing combined reflections.

A *double-sided reflection* captures the ambivalence of a participant about a situation or a course of action. An example would be: "You are feeling really frustrated with your job, but afraid that if you quit, you won't be able to find another one."

Two more advanced types of reflection are *amplification* and *understatement*. In amplification, the worker overstates or exaggerates what a participant has said. An example might be: "So you're saying that if this job search doesn't work, you will never be able to get a job." The amplified reflection may cause the person to back away from the position, belief, or reason for a course of action. If the participant does agree with the amplified reflection, it is a good indication that he or she is serious about this. Similarly, in an understated reflection, the participant has to assert whether the worker has correctly understood the level of commitment (Miller and Rollnick, 2013).

Workers need to be aware of the cultural aspects of reflections. In some cases in some cultures, reflections of feelings can come across as prying. Reflections that develop empathy will be explored in Chapter 8.

Summaries and affirmations

Summaries are a form of reflection used to recap and synthesize a longer period of time during an interview or conversation, as compared to the briefer period of time paraphrased in the reflections discussed above. According to William Miller and Stephen Rollnick (Rosengren, 2009), the founders of Motivational Interviewing, summaries are valuable in that they help participants organize their experience.

Summarizing also can be useful in transitioning from one topic to another. If the worker believes a participant is "spinning his wheels," covering the same ground over and over again, a summary of the participant's statements and/or feelings can lead to a discussion of other topics.

Summaries are also connected to the following skill—using affirmations. When a participant has detailed all the efforts she has made to keep her third-grade son in the same school in spite of having to move from place to place, the worker could summarize the participant's actions, then lead to the affirmation: "You showed the kind of active concern and advocacy that few people could manage."

Affirmations are statements and nonverbal communication that recognize and acknowledge behaviors and actions that lead to positive change. The affirmation may be related to a major step forward or to something as small as positively acknowledging a participant's getting to the appointment on time when traffic was heavy. Affirmations are important because often participants have been ground down by life events and demoralized when they were unable to make things better for themselves and for others close to them. Affirmations, especially when we reframe difficulties as personal strengths, are clear applications of the strengths principle.

Examples of affirmations:

1) I appreciate the effort that you made to meet with me today, given that you had child-care problems.
2) That's a good idea; I would not have thought of that.
3) I am impressed that you managed to hold onto a job with all your unexpected family responsibilities.
4) You handled yourself well in that situation.
5) You clearly have the ability to keep your head in a time of crisis.

Using affirmations requires a level of skill. Participants may react negatively if they feel they are being judged or patronized. As will be discussed in Chapter 8, being genuine is essential. To avoid participants' negative reactions, Rosengren (2009, p. 62) recommends that workers:

1) Focus on specific behaviors whenever possible.
2) Focus on description and not evaluation.
3) Attend to nonproblem areas rather than problem areas.
4) Think of affirmations as crediting interesting qualities to participants.
5) Nurture a strengths-based view of participants instead of a deficit worldview.

Self-disclosure

Workers constructively sharing some of their personal experiences, behaviors, and feelings with participants can be appropriate and valuable. However, when working with a participant, it is a skill to know when to share parts of one's own life and what aspects, past and present, are inappropriate to share.

Major John Cheydleur, a therapist and former Eastern Territorial Social Services Secretary, warned about using self-disclosure too early in working with participants. Workers talking about how they have overcome problems may seem to trivialize the participant's problems or communicate, "I got through this problem—why can't you?" (1999, p. 12). Another danger of self-disclosure is that it can put the focus on the worker rather than on the participant. When workers share too much about their lives, it becomes more difficult to shift back to the participant's life situation.

For a variety of reasons, workers may choose to use self-disclosure to:

1) Reduce the social distance between worker and participant.
2) Model appropriate behavior, as in alcohol and treatment groups.
3) Provide reference points for behavior.
4) Challenge the participant.
5) Share positive feedback regarding participants' strengths and growth.
6) Answer the question, "What would you do?"

Self-disclosure can reduce the social distance between worker and participant.

A worker's life and that of the participant with whom he or she is working may have similarities. Remarking on a similarity can help the participant see the worker as a "real person," not just as a formal helper. It can help the worker establish connections and a stronger relationship. If a participant remarks that her son never can find his shoes in the morning, and the worker happens to be a parent with an absent-minded child, the worker might remark: "My child's just the same way!"

Self-disclosure can be used to provide reference points for behavior.

A worker's own experiences can be used to "normalize" a stressful situation for a participant. When a participant talks about how trying her first week on a new job was, the worker might say, "I remember the first week I worked a job; I thought I would never figure it out—but I did!"

Self-disclosure can be used to challenge the participant.

When a solid professional relationship exists between the worker and participant, and the worker has concerns about a choice or decision the participant is making, the concern may be most honestly voiced in self-disclosure. The worker might say, "Tony, I've been working with you for six months now, and I'm impressed with how well you're doing. I need to tell you I'm concerned about what you're planning to do next week, because I'm afraid it'll really set you back."

Self-disclosure can be used to share positive feedback regarding the participants' strengths and growth.

When a participant is doing well in a situation, the worker may personalize the remarks. The worker might say, "I want to tell you how impressed I am with the way you're juggling work and your family. You know, not many parents could carry it off as well as you're doing."

Self-disclosure can be used to answer the question, "What would you do?"

It can be difficult when a participant asks: *"What would you do in this situation?"* At times, the question can be deflected with a response such as "Let's focus back on your situation." However, at times participants may find that kind of answer evasive. In those cases, the worker might say, "I've never been in that situation, and I tend to make decisions based on my past experiences (followed by a brief description of life experiences). I'm not sure my speculating would do you a lot of good. What have you done when you've been faced with something like this before?" *The complexity of giving advice is also discussed in Chapter 11.*

Tips on using self-disclosure:

1) Make sure your disclosures are appropriate, not only to the subject but also to the timing (what is the participant ready for?).
2) Keep your disclosures selective, focused, and as short as possible.
3) Do not overburden the participant; a participant with a "full plate of problems" may interpret the self-disclosure as the worker sharing more problems.
4) After the self-disclosure, focus back on the participant with a question or statement.

As stated earlier, the stronger the relationship with the participant, the more appropriate it is to use self-disclosure. A worker who is a Christian may be working with a woman who has made clear her Christian faith is important to her. In that situation, it could be appropriate to use the self-disclosure, "When I've been worried about similar situations, I've found that taking it to the Lord in prayer helps." In a situation in which the participant had not already disclosed about her faith, this form of self-disclosure could come across as intrusive and inappropriate.

What not to do

Having good intentions and caring about people is important in this work. However, helping is a skill, and well-intentioned workers can fail to be effective. Below are some common mistakes made in working with people:

1) Moralizing, preaching, sermonizing.
2) Solving problems or giving advice prematurely.
3) Sympathizing and giving cliché responses.
4) Assuming we completely understand.
5) Apologizing for addressing sensitive issues.
6) Arguing with participants.

Moralizing, preaching, sermonizing

When workers have strong values that guide their lives, there is a tendency to want to apply them in looking at the participants' issues. Workers at times use "shoulds" and "oughts," such as "You shouldn't have said that" or "You ought to pay your bills first." Participants have likely heard many "should" and "ought" messages in their lives from family and significant others to make them feel guilty. When they hear from a worker "You should. . . ," the same feelings of guilt and resentment can arise. The participant may also get the message, "You're not smart enough to figure this out, so I (the worker) will tell you what to do." The participant may become defensive, not hear anything else the worker says, and not trust the worker enough to share essential information (Hepworth, Larson, and Rooney, 1997).

Solving problems or giving advice prematurely

There is an important distinction between information and advice. Participants often need information. Whether working with participants regularly in ongoing programing or on a one-time basis for material assistance, workers have an opportunity to share information that may be valuable—the existence of Twelve Step or other recovery groups in the community, how to apply for housing subsidies, etc. However, sharing information is different from giving advice or suggesting solutions to the participant's dilemmas. If the advice is unsolicited, especially if the participant doesn't know the worker well, the participant may view the worker as a know-it-all, and may react defensively. For example, a participant complains about her teenage daughter, and the worker replies: "I think it would be best to try a new approach with your daughter. Let me suggest ______________." The participant may very well react negatively.

Workers also can make the mistake of suggesting potential solutions before listening to and understanding the complexity of the participant's situation. Sometimes new workers will jump in, trying to solve a problem as soon as the participant begins to explain the situation. Questions like "Why don't you go to Community Action and see if they can help you?" are not usually helpful, especially when the questions are asked before knowing what participants have done to try to resolve the situation. Workers who frequently offer unsolicited advice may then develop the habit of giving "canned responses" to participants, passing along the same generic solutions indiscriminately. *In Chapter 11, effective approaches to providing information will be discussed.*

Assuming we completely understand

A participant is talking about the multiple struggles in her life, and the worker asks if there is support from her family. If she says, "My family's pretty close," the worker still does not know how much daily, weekly, or monthly contact there is between family members. The worker also doesn't know how much help and support is offered and provided within that family. Another participant, whose mother recently died and who just lost her job, answers your question, "How are you coping with all that's happened?" with the response, "I'm doing all right." The worker doesn't know from that brief response whether the woman is coping well or whether she's thinking of committing suicide only some of the time.

Sympathizing and giving cliché responses

When someone is in pain, because of the loss of a close family member or because of a traumatic event, it is easy to reply with a cliché or old saying such as "Don't worry. Things will work out" or "Time heals all wounds."

As workers, we reply in these ways for various reasons. We may be too busy to attend to the grief and pain—other people are waiting to see us after we talk to this person. We may be overwhelmed by the situation and don't know how to respond. The person's situation may also tap into the workers' own hurts and unhealed wounds.

Glib responses such as "Don't

worry" may help the workers deal with their own lack of comfort in the situation, but they are not of value to the participant. For someone who has suddenly lost a loved family member, the statement "Time heals all wounds" simply does not seem possible in that moment. When participants hear a superficial or insincere comment, they know the worker doesn't understand their situation and probably will not be of much help.

We can show we understand and care by reflecting not only the content of their issues but also the emotional aspect of their struggles.

Apologizing for addressing sensitive issues

It is necessary at times to talk with participants or applicants for services about issues that are sensitive—alcohol or drug use, self-destructive behavior, or past criminal activity. Workers often feel uncomfortable bringing up these matters; they don't want to seem to be blaming, or they are unsure how the participant will react. However, when workers decide they need to raise sensitive issues and then begin by apologizing for bringing up the subject, they can be ineffective. The focus is then on the worker's apology or reluctance to talk about the issue, not the issue itself.

Arguing with participants

Workers should avoid arguing with participants. Trying to directly persuade participants to take a course of action rarely works. Participants' most common response to workers suggesting or insisting on a course of action is to become more defensive and perhaps get locked into their position. Persuasion is likely to lead to resistance, either openly or silently (Rosengren, 2009). As will be discussed in later chapters, it is far more productive to help the participant to describe both the pros and cons of a possible decision; in essence, we can facilitate getting the participant to argue with himself/herself.

Conclusion

Selecting the right approach is akin to a skilled craftsman who knows the right tool for the job.

The skills and approaches described in this chapter can be applied in a variety of settings and stages in working with individuals and families. Similarly, the "what not to do" section provides examples of practices to avoid while working with participants. Selecting the right approach is akin to the situation of a skilled craftsman or carpenter who knows how to choose the right tool for the job.

Reflection questions

1) How can you use more open questions and fewer closed questions (pages 70-72) in initial interviews and still get the necessary information?

2) When do you find the use of reflections (pages 73, 74) helpful in your work?

3) Could using more affirmations (pages 74, 75) be effective in your work? How?

PART III

Working with Individuals, Families, and Communities

CHAPTER 8

Engagement

"Engagement" is the process by which the worker and participant establish a helpful connection and a working relationship (Miller and Rollnick, 2013). This begins within seconds of when they meet and continues over the course of their working together. Engagement can be seen as the first step in the Stages in Working With Individuals and Families, but Engagement is also an ongoing process.—see Figure 8.1:

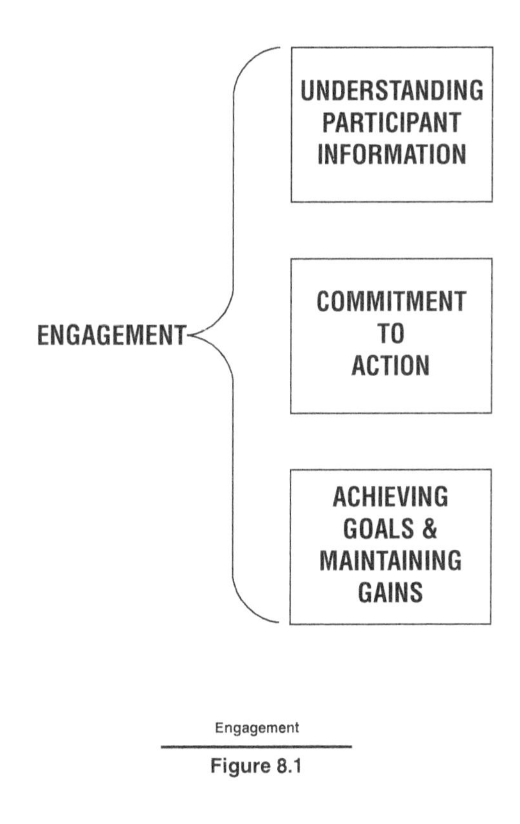

Figure 8.1

Engagement may be especially important when the worker has had prior contact with a participant who was challenging or unsuccessful.

The worker can do a number of things to build a good professional relationship with participants. Among these are demonstrating empathy, creating rapport, being dependable but flexible, responding quickly to participants' changing need priorities, and assessing participants' often-changing needs for intensive services or personal space. Also, workers need to be aware of their own biases in working with participants.

Empathy and rapport

Empathy, rapport, and trust are related concepts. Rapport is a condition in which there is a level of understanding and comfort between worker and participant. This occurs when a participant perceives the worker's helpful intent and comprehension of the situation. This leads to building trust.

Empathy and Engagement

Empathy can be defined as understanding (to some degree) the situation of another and communicating that understanding back to the other person. Making the effort to be empathetic demonstrates caring. Participants can sense when workers care about them and wish to help them with their concerns.

Research has shown the value of empathy. "The skill of acknowledging the participant's feelings appeared to contribute substantially to the development of a good working relationship between worker and participant as well as contributing to the worker's ability to be helpful" (Shulman, 1999). When one can understand a person's situation from his/her perspective, then it is possible to convey an understanding of how those circumstances uniquely affect the person involved.

Often there can be confusion between sympathy and empathy. When a worker expresses to a participant, "I'm so sorry about what happened to you," she is sharing her feelings. However, this is sympathy, not empathy. It reflects the worker's feelings, which may or may not be those of the participant. When the worker says, "Sounds like things are pretty tough for you these days," or "You're really excited about all the changes in your life," she is attempting to convey her understanding of the world from the participant's vantage point."

Empathy is a two-stage process. It involves listening carefully to the participant's words and observing nonverbal communication to gain understanding, then communicating that comprehension back to the participant. In Chapter 7, the use of reflections is described. Reflections are a very effective way of showing empathy.

Building rapport with participants

Rapport is fostered in a number of ways. It starts with the first impression the worker makes with the participant. Research studies have shown that people form judgments of those they see or meet in as little as a tenth of a second (Willis and Todorov, 2006). Studies also indicate that participants depend on the following nonverbal behaviors of practitioners to determine whether or not the workers are hearing and respecting them:

1) A tone of voice that matches the participant's.
2) Eye contact.
3) Occasional head nodding to show that the worker is attending to what the participant says.
4 Varying facial expressions in response to what the participant says.
5) Smiling at appropriate points to demonstrate warmth and understanding.
6) Occasional hand gesturing.
7) Sitting in close physical proximity to participants.
8) Using a moderate rate of speech.
9) Leaning slightly towards the participant to indicate interest and concentration (Okun, 1992).

When workers treat participants with dignity, are nonjudgmental, and value the participants' abilities and right to self-determination, rapport can be established (Hepworth, Larson, and Rooney, 1997).

Berg and Miller (1992) touch on the relationship between worker and participant from the perspective of therapy, but there is application to other helping work:

> The traditional emphasis on obtaining the cooperation of the participant is, however, hopelessly one-sided and, therefore, does not constitute cooperation at all. In fact, cooperation, as routinely described by treatment professionals, is analogous to a therapeutic *Animal Farm,* in which the rule is that all participants in therapy must cooperate equally, but some participants must cooperate more equally than others—the latter referring chiefly to the participant. In the "intervention" process described above no attempt is made to see the problem from the participant's perspective, to speak his or her own language, to work within his or her unique frame of reference, to negotiate a mutually agreeable treatment goal, or to use existing strengths and resources in an effort to solve the problem. The entire process is based on the idea that the participant is "delusional" and "out of touch with reality" and must be forced to "cooperate" with the treatment as recommended. Co-

> operation, as Sesame Street's *Big Bird* is so fond of pointing out, means working together with one another. Therefore, in a truly co-operative therapeutic relationship, not only must the participant co-operate by working with the worker, but the worker must co-operate by working with the participant (p. 15).

Relationships that are to some degree reciprocal can build trust. Workers are "one-up" on participants in that by the nature of their relationship they have more power. However, the relationship becomes more reciprocal when the worker asks, for example, what strategies the participant used to avoid harm in living on the streets. At that moment, the participant is the teacher, and the worker is the student. The switching of roles reduces, at least temporarily, that power imbalance and can lead to more trust.

Approaches for building trust

Being dependable but flexible

One of the difficulties in forming and maintaining relationships with people seeking assistance from The Salvation Army is that a large number of them have had at least one unsatisfactory experience with a worker. When asking participants what was problematic about their relationship, participants often say: "She (or he) didn't do what they said they were going to ."

One review on case management programs with those in homeless situations found that homeless people are more interested in services that provide tangible benefits than in treatment or learning daily living skills. This suggests that case management programs start by offering basic, concrete services before moving on to longer-range or clinical services (Mercier, 1995).

Providing concrete help may be useful in several ways. Obviously, the material aid can be helpful to the individual or family. Additionally, providing resources can demonstrate that the workers can be of real assistance and will follow through consistently on what they have stated they will do. Another positive aspect of providing concrete help is that it may offer an opportunity for genuine conversation that may be more productive than time spent talking in an office. As one worker stated, "I usually don't take participants grocery shopping or to do their laundry. However, when I do, I find that I can get more work done with participants while we are folding their laundry than talking in any other setting (Cutshall, 1996)."

Especially for some participants

who have trouble trusting, workers need to be very clear in communicating what they will and will not do. In cases where participants are very needy and/or would prefer the worker do most of the work, the participants may interpret any mention of possible assistance as a "promise." When this does not occur, the participants interpret it as another instance in which unresponsive and undependable workers let them down. As will be detailed in Chapter 10, writing what the *participant* will do and what the worker will do in the coming week is necessary not only for accountability purposes but also to prevent misunderstanding.

The importance of being genuine, of coming across as a real person and not just as someone in the role of a worker, cannot be overstated. One worker demonstrates genuineness by showing participants blank copies of the forms she is filling out and tells them: "Look, I know that this is a lot of questions, but the government wants us to collect this information. And that means we get to have this program, and I get to do this job."

Responding quickly to participants' changing needs and priorities

As stated in the section on self-determination in Chapter 3, people generally are more committed to and put more energy into goals and plans they make, rather than ones imposed on them. However, plans and goals change, as do the needs of participants. Workers cannot assume that after the initial assessment and goal setting they fully understand the participants' situation and priorities. Crises happen and priorities shift.

Conclusion

Overcoming our biases is important for our work.

Much of this chapter has been concerned with the participants' expectations of workers, their biases regarding them, and approaches for overcoming these so that a strong work relationship can be formed and maintained. However, there also are situations in which workers have negative perceptions and biases about participants. The biases may be related to race and ethnicity, but they may also be based on having had a prior negative experience with a participant.

Current Salvation Army workers in Wisconsin were asked how they overcame their biases when working with participants who had not followed through in the past when they sought help from the Army. Here are some of their answers (Community-Based Learning Class, 2014):

1) "How do we look past what has happened before and start over? Just remind yourself you really never know when they come into the building if it's actually going to be a time they're ready to change."
2) "If they were discharged from the shelter for rules violations—like drinking—and a couple of years later we let them come back, I'm not going to hold the past against them, but I will keep an extra eye out for the drinking. I try to treat everyone like it's the first time."
3) "I talk about it. I'll say: 'Let's start over, ' and this lets the participant know I am not judging them. However, I will still bring up things when I know the person could be working harder, even if I know they don't want to hear this from me."
4) "I have to kind of wipe my brain clean of what they have done in the past. Just try to see the face of Jesus in everyone who comes in."

Reflection questions

1) Think of one or more times when you have had good rapport (page 87) with a participant. What did you do to make this happen? What difference did it make?
2) On page 90 are examples of approaches Salvation Army workers have used to overcome their own bias in working with participants. What do you do to be effective with participants with whom you have had negative experiences in the past?

CHAPTER 9

Understanding the Situation of Participants: Current Challenges, Aspirations, Strengths, and Readiness to Change

In social work and human services, there has been an evolution in terms describing the stage when a situation or problem is introduced. Until the 1960s, social workers primarily used the term "diagnosis," borrowed from the medical profession. Problems were viewed as illnesses or diseases based within a patient.

In the past half-century, the term "assessment" has been commonly used to describe the process by which a worker evaluates a situation to acquire an understanding of what caused a problem and what can be changed to minimize its impact or to resolve it (Kirst-Ashman and Hull, 2012). "Assessment" sounds as if a worker does something to a participant, primarily concerned with understanding human flaws and frailty. Until recently, it has focused almost entirely on what's wrong with the ways participants manage life situations and crises (Weick and Saleebey, 1998).

Focusing only on understanding problems and what has gone wrong leads to a problem-saturated description of the situation. As Saleebey points out, "Schizophrenia is real. Child sexual abuse is real. Pancreatic cancer is real. Violence is real. But in the lexicon of strengths, it is as wrong to deny the possible as it is to deny the problem" (1996, p. 297). However, if an assessment is largely about deficits and problems, these are likely to be the focus of the worker and the participant.

How do we think about the presenting situation of participants? Motivational Interviewing uses the term "conversations about change," instead of "interview" or "meeting," and there is merit in thinking about our interactions this way. Conversations about change can help participants define their situations and assist them in evaluating and giving meaning to factors that affect them (Saleebey, 1997). When this happens, the likelihood increases that the worker, and often the participant, will gain an understanding of how doing something differently could lead to substantial progress.

Compare the following two approaches to understanding a participant's situation. In one, the assessment consists of a list of questions the worker wants the participant to answer. The questions include, "When did you last work?" and "Have you sought help from your family?" Although all the questions may yield valuable information, they combine to put participants on the defensive. Participants then may be unlikely to say anything that could hinder their chances of getting help.

In contrast, the worker can engage the person seeking help by carefully listening to the story the participant wishes to tell. By using a number of techniques to understand the nature of the challenges the participants face, the worker can learn about the participants' resources, strengths, hopes, and readiness to make changes. In this process, the worker will use the techniques and approaches discussed in Chapter 7, asking far more open than closed questions. The worker also will use reflections to check understanding and communicate empathy.

In this and following stages of the process, workers need to listen to the participants' language for "change talk." Coming out of Motivational Interviewing, change talk is defined as any self-expressed language of the participants that is an argument for change (Miller and Rollnick, 2013, p. 159). The degree of change talk is an indication of the participants' current level of motivation.

Understanding participants through the lenses of culture and class, their worldview, and their past

Knowing that a participant has a history of alcoholism does not fully inform a worker about the meaning of alcohol and drinking in the participant's life. The importance of culture in understanding participants' situations is discussed in Chapter 6. Cultural belief systems and expected behaviors influence people's ideas, customs, and skills. Their norms, customs, and traditions can be valuable resources or can become obstacles to effective functioning and reaching goals (Lum, 1996).

As also stated in Chapter 6, knowing the race and/or ethnic background of individuals does not mean workers understand how the individuals view their present situation. It may be important to find out the relative importance of race/ethnicity to participants and their families and how assimilated they are to mainstream culture. Also, the social and economic class of individuals can influence how they view their present situation and what is likely to happen.

These factors influence the worldview of a person. Goldstein (1984) cautioned us about the importance of seeing participant problems within the context of the person's worldview:

> The notion of a problem is relatively meaningless until we gain some appreciation of where it fits within the pattern of the participant's living, how it is understood and what it means to him or her, what is at stake either in perpetuating or changing the problem, and whether a solution is possible. As a "problem," the abuse that the battered woman has suffered so long takes on radically different meanings when she finally concludes that all hope for the future of the relationship is lost and that an alternative way of life is either necessary or possible. The alcoholics' "problem" doesn't really exist as far as they are concerned until their illusions no longer serve them and another solution is called for (p. 284).

Asking the participant to clarify the meaning and impact of a problematic situation can help the worker's understanding. There is a major difference between a participant saying "I'm an alcoholic" and "Here are the ways my drinking has hurt me and the it has messed up my life." The worker can come to understand the issue in context by asking such questions as: "How does this situation negatively affect you?" and "What's the worst thing about this situation?"

Understanding a participant's situations in the context of their life experience can give the worker valuable information about successful functioning. Remember, when workers first meet participants, it may be at one of the low points of their life. At other times (perhaps at most other times) they functioned well. However, when we first meet someone, there is a tendency to assume their present situation is an extension of how things have always been.

Asking about the past can also lead to an understanding of strategies the participants may have used that worked for them then. In talking with a participant with a long history of alcohol abuse who went on a three-day binge after having been sober for five months, the worker can ask, "How did you keep from drinking during all those months?" Careful exploration of the participant's strategies when cravings were strong and later when depression may have set in can help the participant and the worker become more aware of the participant's coping styles. This awareness, and being able to "name and claim" the strategies, can aid the participant in current efforts to resist drinking (Berg and Miller, 1992).

It is also valuable to inquire about what the participant has already tried, to find out what worked and what didn't. When participants are depressed, suicidal, or overwhelmed, the worker asks questions such as:

1) When you were confronted in the past with this issue, how did you cope?
2) What ways of dealing with the issue were successful (at least for a while)?
3) What else have you found to be helpful?

Exploring the past can also help participants see the part of them that has been and is healthy. Although their lives contain pain and disappointment, as in other lives, they contain a history of achievement (Rapp, 1998, p. 91).

Solution-focused approaches (also referred to as solution-oriented) emphasize what is happening now and how it could be changed. Understanding why there are problems or what is wrong is not central to this approach. In working with participants with mental health issues, with families involved with Child Protective Services, and with those struggling with addiction, practitioners using this approach asked questions that yielded possibilities and moved towards solutions.

They recommend asking early in an initial interview or conversation: "What have you tried?" Participants' answers give workers a sense of what steps the participants have taken, their actual and potential strengths, where they have been successful, and the obstacles they may have encountered.

Looking for exceptions can be productive. One can ask about times when a particular concern was not present, when things were better. Questions that are useful in helping participants think of exceptions include:

1) When you had trouble getting out of bed last week, what did you do that got you going?
2) When in the past several weeks has this issue or problem been less severe?
3) What is different about those times?
4) What happens instead?
5) Who does what differently? You and family members/friends?
6) What will have to be different for this to happen more often?
7) Who is most likely to do things differently? Explain.
8) How will you know when things are really better?

(DeJong and Berg, 1998).

Helping participants view their situation through the lens of the strengths perspective

At the start of this chapter and in Chapter 3, the importance of workers looking for participants' strengths was emphasized. However, participants often do not recognize strengths they already possess. Identifying these can lead to their becoming confident about being able to reach their goals. Listed below are a number of strengths in the areas of cognition, emotion, motivation, coping, and interpersonal relations:

Cognition

1) Sees the world as most other people in that culture see it.
2) Has an understanding of right and wrong from that cultural and ethnic perspective.
3) Understands how one's behavior affects others and how one is affected by others; is insightful.
4) Is open to different ways of thinking about things.
5) Reasoning is easy to follow.
6) Considers and weighs alternatives in problem solving.

Emotion

1) Is in touch with feelings and is able to express them if encouraged.
2) Expresses love and concern for others.
3) Demonstrates a degree of self-control.
4) Can handle stressful situations reasonably well.
5) Is positive about life and has hope.
6) Has a range of emotions.

7) Emotions are appropriate to the situation.

Motivation

1) When having problems, doesn't hide from, avoid, or deny them.
2) Willing to seek help and share problem situation when there is trust.
3) Willing to accept responsibility for own part or role in issues or life difficulties.
4) Wants to improve current and future situations.
5) Does not want to be dependent on others.
6) Seeks to improve self through further knowledge, education, and skill development.

Coping

1) Persistent in handling crises and ongoing difficulties.
2) Is well-organized.
3) Follows through on decisions.
4) Is resourceful and creative with limited resources.
5) Stands up for self rather than submitting to injustice.
6) Attempts to pay debts despite financial difficulty.
7) Prepares for and handles new situations well.
8) Has dealt successfully with related problems in the past.

Interpersonal Relations

1) Has friends.
2) Seeks to understand friends, family members, and others.
3) Makes sacrifices for friends, family members, and others.
4) Performs social roles appropriately (for example, parental, spouse, son or daughter, community).
5) Is outgoing and friendly.
6) Is truthful.
7) Is cooperative and flexible in relating to family and friends.
8) Is self-confident in relationships with others.
9) Shows warm acceptance of others.
10) Can accept loving and caring feelings from others.

Faith, religion, and spirituality as strengths

As was stated in Chapter 2, for many individuals their spirituality and/or religious practices are a source of support. The process of knowing the participant's situation should include understanding the religious/spiritual orientation, the degree of their religious affiliations and most important, the meaning these have for them. In many cases, the religious/spiritual life of participants is central to who they are.

Many workers are reluctant to ask about religious or spiritual beliefs or practices. Students in a graduate social work class were asked to write about the role of religion and spirituality in their practice. Here is an excerpt from one student's paper:

> At my (field) placement I don't know if participants bring their view of God into discussions with me because this will make them seem like "good participants," that this is what they are supposed to do to successfully complete the program, or if God is really that primary in their lives. It makes me a little bit uncomfortable, like I'm supposed to say something in agreement or nod and smile, but God forbid (!) should I say I don't agree. My mother always told me, it's best to avoid discussing religion and politics (Jackson, 1996).

The student is voicing her discomfort at mentioning God, at welcoming spiritual and religious dynamics in the helping encounter. Her uneasiness is not unique. Many workers, including those whose own Christian faith is strong, are reluctant to bring up matters of faith, religion, and spirituality, often because they don't want to appear to be forcing their beliefs on participants.

A conversation about change will allow participants to share their problems and strengths and to talk about their faith and beliefs. The worker can then understand the strengths spiritually-based participants bring to the assessment and goal-setting process. These can include values of right/wrong and a clear sense of one's roles and responsibilities (Pellebon and Anderson, 1999).

Approaches that incorporate the spiritual and religious aspects of people's lives include inviting open questions and social support maps. Such as:

1) What gives meaning to your life?
2) What are your greatest sources of strength?
3) Who do you turn to in times of great trouble?

Participants may answer these in secular terms, talking about their parents or children as those who support them and help in hard times. Others may answer the question "Who do you turn to in times of great trouble?" with "My Lord and Savior Jesus, who will always be by my side." For participants for whom religion and faith are important, open questions such as the above can open the door to bring their faith, beliefs, and practices into the conversation.

If the individual is religious, it may be important to know to what degree the problem is given a religious interpretation and the degree to which religion is used as a control mechanism (Denton, 1990). Religious beliefs are a framework through which we experience and interpret life events. Religious beliefs may be intertwined with ethnic or cultural background. "Families who are Baptist or Jehovah's Witness, for example, are likely to derive very different types of comfort from their religious beliefs in dealing with the death of a child from Sudden Infant Death Syndrome" (Van Hook, 1998, p. 191).

When faith-based programs such as those of The Salvation Army receive federal funding, there are requirements that need to be followed:

> Some of the legal obligations that come along with a Federal government grant include the responsibility to separate any explicitly religious activities from programs funded by direct government grants. Explicitly religious activities (activities that involve overt religious content, such as religious instruction, devotional exercises, worship, proselytizing, or evangelism) must be clearly separated in either time or location from the federally funded program. These religious activities also must be privately funded and purely voluntary for program beneficiaries. Organizations receiving Federal funds may not discriminate against beneficiaries or prospective beneficiaries on the basis of religion or religious belief. Further, if a beneficiary or prospective beneficiary objects to the religious character of an organization providing federally funded services, the beneficiary must be referred to an alternative provider. (Office of Faith-Based and Neighborhood Programs, 2015).

Understanding the social support system of participants

There is an old Irish proverb: "We live in the shelter of each other." For many of us, this is true, and our family, friends, and other people important in our lives are our largest source of support. In understanding the situation of participants, it is crucial to understand those persons in the context of their social support systems.

Social support maps (also referred to as eco-maps) are drawings that place an individual or family within a social context. As illustrated in Figure 9.1, the participant will identify real and potential social supports in the following areas: family, friends, neighbors, people from work or school, clubs or organizations, formal helpers, and churches

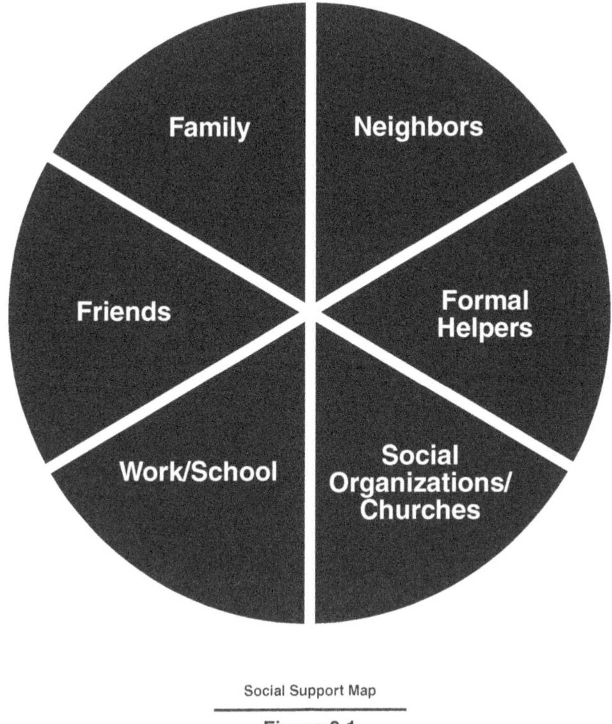

Social Support Map

Figure 9.1

and spiritual support.

For each of the "pieces of the pie," ask participants to start from the middle of the circle and near that box put the person or source of support most important to them. Continue moving outward in the circle until they have listed the significant people/places in their life where they find support. If there is conflict or tension in any of these relationships, underline the name of that person or organization with a wavy line.

These maps usually are drawn jointly by the worker and participants and help both to view the participants in the context of their social world. This tool can be useful not only in assessment but also in planning and in helping participants progress towards a preferred future. Staff can use the process and information at some point to engage participants in discussions of how to reach out and use identified social supports.

One caution in using social support maps and other mapping techniques is that the worker may automatically equate family with support. Some participants come from families with limited resources.

Some families of origin are beset by multiple problems. Because of substance abuse, family violence, and other issues, family members are not resources at this time, and contact at present with family may be strained or harmful (Sheafor, Horejsi, and Horejsi, 1994, p. 269).

Participants, especially those with severe mental illness and/or a long history of substance abuse, may have lost contact with their former social environment. When the lives of participants revolve around shelters, day programs for those in homeless situations, and specialized mental health programs, their daily contact is limited to those with similar difficulties and to professionals. They may not have the kinds of contact with the larger world—including businesses, social and recreational opportunities, and extended family members—that we rely on to stimulate and enrich us (Rapp, 1998).

When we ask about what has worked in the past and inquire about interests and aspirations, we can find out about possible connections to the larger world.

Readiness to change

Another important element in understanding the situation of participants is comprehending how ready and/or motivated they are to make changes at this point in their life.

In Chapter 5, the Stages of Change in the Transtheoretical Model was presented. This model conceptualizes change as a number of stages that require changes in attitude in order to progress. The model depicts change as a cyclical process as opposed individuals continually progress (Prochaska and DiClemente, 1982). The authors contend that it is quite normal for people to require several trips through the stages to make lasting change. So in this sense, reaching goals and then slipping back is viewed as a normal part of the change process, as opposed to failure. This does not mean this kind of relapse is desirable or even always to be expected. It simply means change is difficult and that it is unreasonable to expect everyone to be able to modify a habit perfectly without any slips.

Much depends on where participants are in the Stages of Change Model. We have all seen individuals in the Pre-Contemplation Stage, who are so accustomed to their present situation that it does not seem problematic. Many alcoholics are in the Pre-Contemplation Stage. Some participants who are used to housing instability find housing, hold on to it for a few months, get

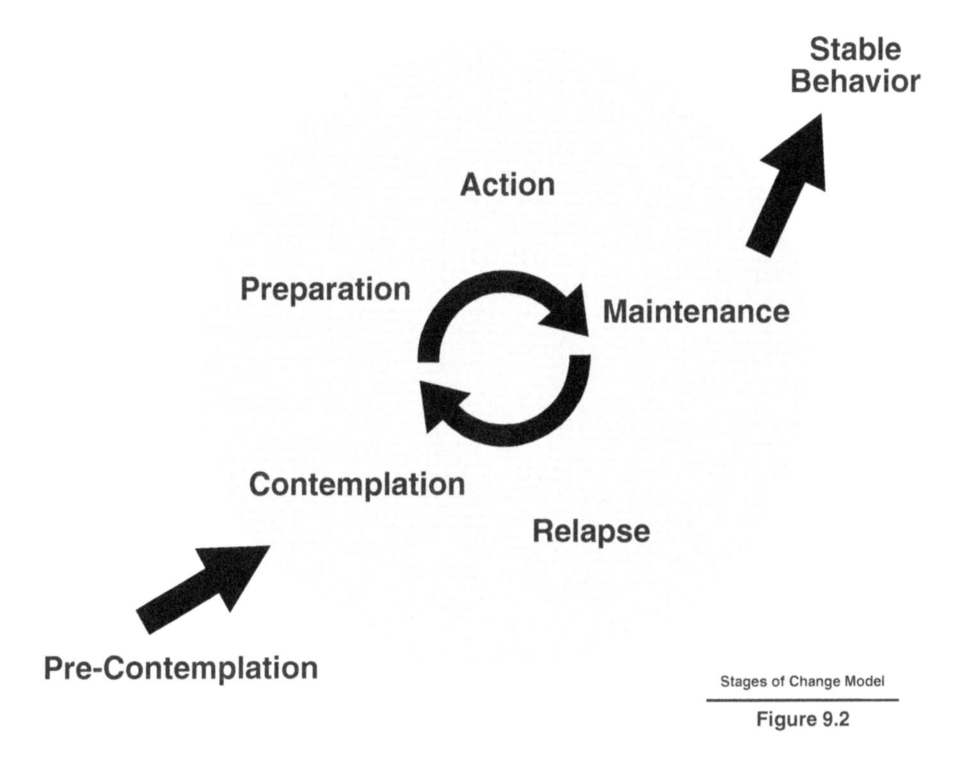

Stages of Change Model

Figure 9.2

evicted, and end up in a shelter again. It may be they are so discouraged that breaking the cycle does not seem possible, and they feel "stuck in the eternal present."

In situations like these, the role of the worker is to engage the participant in looking at the difficulties that arise in the present situation, so that the participant may begin to consider doing something different. Trying to persuade someone to take action when they do not see their behavior or choices as problematic almost never works. Trying to set goals for change will be fruitless.

Some participants, however, are in the Contemplation Stage, in which taking action seems the way to go, but it is unclear how to get there. In both cases, looking at the present in the context of a different and better future may lead to action.

Understanding the situation in the context of a preferred future

When people are without hope, they are missing one of their strongest allies. Programs for persons in homeless situations, for example, often concentrate on helping persons achieve permanent housing and secure a job and/or benefits sufficient to maintain their housing.

It is easy for participants (and sometimes workers) to focus on problems and on how difficult things are. Very often participants talk about their problems in ways that give little indication of how they would like their lives to look when their problems are solved or partly solved. Talking about actions that can make things better—*solution talk*—can counteract the sense of powerlessness (DeJong and Berg, 1998).Asking such questions as "How are things going to be different for you after you leave here with a Section 8 voucher?" can help focus the participant on the actions needed to escape homelessness and also on a life that could be, in the participant's own terms, better.

Conclusion

Understanding a participant's situation helps in planning for a different and better future.

Understanding the situation of a participant—through exploration of culture and worldview, the role of faith and religion, the support system and readiness to change—can help the worker and participant in planning for a different and better future.

Reflection questions

1) How does understanding participants' situations in the context of their life experiences (pages 93, 94) help us to comprehend their situation more fully?

2) In your work how do you build on the strengths of participants (pages 95, 96)?

3) What other approaches from this chapter would be useful?

CHAPTER 10

Commitment to Action: Planning and Setting Goals

When a participant is considering a future that is different from and better than the present in at least one way, the worker can assist in turning what is often a vague idea into plans that can be acted on. Three interrelated parts of this process are imagining the better future, developing commitment to change, and formulating a specific plan of action.

In *Faith in Action,* the planned change or case management process is explained as a linear process. As discussed in the previous chapter, we start with understanding/assessment. We then use that information for goal planning, proceed to achieving goals and maintaining the gains, and transition to not needing services (or as many services). There is logic and purpose to this order. We need to understand the participants' situations in order to assist in goal setting; the specificity of goals is invaluable in the rest of the work.

However, on a day-to-day basis, things are often not as clear. As part of the understanding process, participants can be encouraged to move back and forth between "problem talk and solution talk" (DeJong and Berg, 1995, p. 184). As participants tell what is wrong in their life, workers can ask them to describe how things could be different and better. The process of setting goals and working towards reaching them often yields valuable information for the participants as to their strengths, or they may find the issues are more difficult than anticipated. This new learning may then be incorporated into revision of goals or action steps.

Also, the Stages of Change Model is one in which individuals proceed from being uninterested in changing behaviors or their circumstances to thinking seriously about changing and making dedicated efforts to reach their goals. But in reality all of us experience varying levels of commitment in working for things we consider to be important. Unanticipated challenges and unforeseen obstacles may make progress more difficult. For that reason, the worker needs to continually use techniques and approaches that build and maintain commitment.

In the previous chapter, the concept of *change talk* was introduced. Coming out of Motivational Interviewing, change talk is defined as any self-expressed language that is an argument for change (Miller and Rollnick, 2013, p. 159). The degree of change talk is an indication of the participants' current level of motivation. Different kinds of change talk have been identified.

Preparatory change talk refers to language that the participant uses in his/her own internal arguments for change. The acronym "DARN" is used to identify the four elements of preparatory change talk:

Desire to change
(I want, I would like, I wish).

Ability to change
(I can, I could).

Reasons to change
(if I make this change, then).

Need to change
(I have to, I got to, I need).

Mobilizing change talk signals movement away from ambivalence to putting energy towards making changes. The clearest example of this is *commitment language*, the words we use when we make promises. An example of this is "I will." Another example of commitment language is "I intend to," although that contains a little doubt.

Activation language consists of words that imply commitment to action without actually saying it. Phrases like this signal that the person is moving towards change:

1) "I'm willing to".

2) "I am ready to".

3) "I am prepared to" (Miller and Rollnick, 2013, p. 162).

Taking steps is another type of mobilizing change talk. The worker identifies words the participant is using that show movement towards making changes. An example is a participant telling her worker that she called four places for possible jobs and has been talking to friends who are employed to see if there will be openings where they work.

Working towards a better future

In many circumstances, the worker may decide not to go directly from a present problem to immediately working to resolve it. Rather, taking time to listen to participants' hopes for the future can lead to greater motivation. We encounter people who appear to have lost hope for the future. When we encourage them to dream and plan for the future, powerful things can happen. Participants in a parenting group were asked one November to think about how they would like things to be different in their family by the Fourth of July of the coming year. The participants were all on public assistance and were referred to the parenting group by Child Protective Services.

Some answers were surprising. One woman talked about wanting to enroll in vocational school by that time so that she could get off public assistance. Another mother spoke of a family situation in which she shouted less and her boys were not always fighting.

Asking how things could be different and better creates the opportunity first to think about a preferred reality and then to begin to plan towards desired outcomes. One useful tool for helping participants think of a better future is a worksheet (see following page).

One advantage of using Figure 10.1: Planning for a Better Future (on next page) is that it asks participants not only to rate the importance of positive changes in specific areas of their lives but also to begin to assess how likely or feasible these would be. It's easy to dream of *castillos en el aire,* a Spanish phrase for dreams that have no foundation in reality. The growth of lotteries in recent decades is partly due to the fact that for many working people who see their wages stagnating or reduced, the slim chance of winning the lottery seems the most likely avenue for improving their economic well-being.

Figure 10.1: Planning for a Better Future

Ask participants to think for a minute about how they would like things to be for them (or them and their family) six to nine months from now. Then in the areas below have

Area of Life	How Important?	How Likely?
Scale: 1-10 (Ten is the highest score)		
Housing		
Financial		
Work/Education		
Social Supports		
Physical/ Emotional Health		
Other (Explain)		

Planning for a Better Future

Figure 10.1

them write specifics about what that would be like. This vision of the future should be one in which things are better in some way or ways than they are now. Participants should not base their plan on winning the lottery or inheriting lots of money from a lost great-uncle. Then ask them to rate the areas 1 to 10, 10 being the most important and 1, the least.

Believing in participants' abilities to attain their goals is essential. When people are dispirited, often workers need to believe in them first before they can believe in themselves. This is the social nature of hope. Whether it is in the community of a church, in a support group, or with a few friends, it is easier to have hope in the future when that hope is shared by others.

Before engaging in goal setting

A number of concepts and theories were presented in Chapter 5, and reviewing this material can be useful leading up to working with participants on goal setting.

The Expectancy Theory of Motivation underscores the importance of participants working on goals they see as important to them and attainable. Connected to this is the idea of a Postcard From the Future, discussed in the work of Chip and Dan Heath (see p. 51), noting that a goal connected to a future that is different and better can be motivating.

Also from the work of the Heaths is the concept of Bright Spots, looking for positive exceptions. As mentioned elsewhere, exploring with the participant times when there has been more success can point to workable strategies and goals.

From Motivational Interviewing comes the idea that individuals are motivated to work when with a helper they resolve their ambivalence to change—and this is a process that can continue through the entire time of working with the participant.

The Transtheoretical Theory of Change also provides us with a way to look at the when of change, and a lens to see where individuals are in relation to readiness to commit energy and resources to a change effort. However, a normal part of the change process is moving forward and then slipping back.

Other valuable strategies are related to goal setting. Insoo Kim Berg (1994), who uses a solution-focused approach in family-based interventions for at-risk families, explains why it is preferable to state goals as positive replacement behavior rather than the absence of negative, undesirable behavior:

> A participant saying things like "I will never do it again," "I will never get mad," "I will never let him in," "I will never leave the child alone," is not enough. It is unrealistic to think that she will remember not to do all these things in the heat of anger or frustration. The more concrete, detailed options the participant has, the better. Therefore, you need to clarify the goal with the participant by asking: "So what would you do instead of getting mad (getting drunk, leaving the child alone, etc.)?".... The process of having to describe these alternatives forces participants to think out loud, and thus realistic choices can be made.... It is easier to recognize when a positive goal has been achieved than a negative one. That is, when the participant does not hit the child, it is difficult for her to know that she is not hitting. If she sets herself goals such as "I will count to 10," "I will send him to his room," "I will walk out of the house," she will know when she is achieving her goal (p. 59).

Helping participants with setting goals should include discussing the potential risks and implications as well as the benefits of reaching goals. Berg and Miller (1992) stress that meeting goals involves hard work. An achieved goal that involves hard work is something to be proud of and is a boost to self-esteem.

Participants also need to realize there may be drawbacks in reaching goals and making changes in their lives. People who quit drinking or quit using drugs often find they are not comfortable around old friends who are still using. After successfully making other changes, participants may encounter jealousy by people they know who are not doing as well. Movement towards a better future is usually a challenge, and not always successful. At times, we need to remind participants they are not failures if they do not reach a goal. Taking longer to reach goals than originally planned is also not a sign of weakness.

Goal setting and SMART goals

Goal setting is essential in working with participants. Goal setting not only produces a plan of action that is doable and can be evaluated, but also in the process the participant can develop a clearer idea of priorities and what is possible.

Presented in this chapter is the widely used SMART goals format. SMART goals probably originated with the publication of Ken Blanchard and Spencer Johnson's Leadership and the One-Minute Manager in 1982. Its wide use is at least partially due to the acronym being easy to remember, although the meaning of the letters varies from version to version. The most commonly used version is presented below:

Specific

A specific goal is one that is clear, stating what the result will be and who is going to be involved in reaching the goal. If it is not easily apparent who is responsible, the goal should be rewritten.

Measurable

At times, the goals participants set are stated so broadly that it would be difficult to tell if they have been achieved. When goals are well-stated and it will be evident when they are met, it's easier for participants to measure progress towards the goals. The following goals are those set by participants in Pathway of Hope:

1) Obtain full-time employment as a paralegal before unemployment benefits end.
2) Before the school year starts, sign a lease on a three-bedroom apartment in the Madison School District.
3) Complete GED testing by November 15.

Attainable

Dreams are important. At the same time, the worker may have to help the participants explore goals that are realistic, given their skills, capacities, and life experience. If a woman has had trouble coping with high-stress job situations in the past, the worker may ask her to consider the kind of job environment in which she will not only be successful but also which she might enjoy. If the goal will involve major changes in such aspects as relationships, finances, or ways of managing conflict, the participant needs to consider how likely it is that these changes can be maintained over time.

The extent of the participant's resources is also important in determining how realistic the goals are. Using a strengths perspective, an expanded view of resources can include the support system, past successes in dealing with situations, and other personal capacities and informal community resources. For participants with more resources, meeting ambitious goals may be less difficult than for participants with fewer developed resources and with less support. However, in this process, workers need to be aware of their personal biases and of commonly held stereotypes. Some might assume that participants will not be able to pursue ambitious goals just because of their family background, racial/ethnic heritage, or because they have a disability.

The phrase "Zone of Proximal Development" in psychology refers to the difference between one's current state or situation and what could be possible with effort and support (Vygotsky, 1978). The Zone of Proximal Development is similar to the frequently used term "comfort zone." A poster in a worker's office reads: "Everything you've ever wanted is one step outside your comfort zone." Reaching a goal may involve participants taking a step or two beyond what they have done before. But workers and participants should be cautious about making the goal so big it seems overwhelming and unattainable.

Relevant

It needs to be clear that the goals agreed on are central to the participants' situations. As potential goals are being discussed, check that they directly relate to the issues the participants face as well as fit with their abilities. There can be a tendency to set goals that are easy to reach or do not substantially help the participant deal with issues or get to a better place. The following questions can be useful in deciding among potential goals:

1) Which issue seems to be causing the most pain for the participant?
2) Which issue, if unresolved, will have the most adverse consequences?
3) Which issue, if resolved or managed differently, will have the most desirable outcome for the participant?
4) Which issue can be resolved or managed with moderate investment of time, effort, or other resources? Where do the benefits outweigh the costs?
5) Which issue has the potential of the participant being successful and enhancing competency and mastery? (Locke, Garrison, and Winship, 1998).

Time-bound

Setting a realistic time frame can place an optimum amount of pressure on the participants to achieve goals. If the time frame is too short, the participant may feel it's not possible to reach the goals, and motivation may lag. If the time frame is too long, participants may feel they don't need to get started yet, that they have plenty of time. Finding the balance can be an art. Like the porridge in *Goldilocks and the Three Bears,* it's hard to get it not too hot, not too cold, but just right.

Making sure goals are workable

Goals may fail for a variety of reasons. As stated earlier, the goals may not be the participant's. The goals may be too ambitious given the time frame. They may be stated in terms too vague to be measured, or in professional jargon the participant does not fully understand. Even when the goals are central to the participant, feelings of powerlessness and lack of confidence may cut in and paralyze the participant. The participant may not have the skills at the time to achieve the goal, and it may also be that in the community in which the participant lives there are not the resources for reaching the goal.

An extremely valuable tool for assessing whether goals are workable comes from the work of psychologist Gabriele Oettingen, whose research in the United States and Germany has validated the concept of *mental contrasting* (2014). In mental contrasting, the worker and participant deliberately think about the obstacles and potential setbacks that could occur in trying to achieve a goal, what strategies could be employed to overcome the obstacles, and how likely it would be that the goal would then be successful. Dr. Oettingen found that people whose goals turned out to be realistic were more motivated, and those whose goals were less realistic became less motivated over time. In the cases in which the goals as written were not realistic, they could be retooled or other goals substituted.

Goals may also fail because of worker action and inaction. The goal-setting language—especially being specific and measurable—is initially foreign to workers, and it takes skills and experience to master this. Workers may also have an incomplete picture of participant talents or underestimate their abilities (Rapp, 1998, p. 100).

Goal setting is only the first part of the planning process. When goals are stated clearly and specifically, then the steps the participant needs to take to reach them can be determined. Strategies for holding on to the gains realized in goal achievement also have to be put in place. The use of action steps and other strategies for goal attainment will be described in the following chapter.

Conclusion

"I'll help you solve this yourself!"

The steps and procedures in this chapter are ways to implement the following standards of *The Salvation Army National Social Services Standards Manual:*

4.5.1 The program develops service plans tailored to the needs of each participant.

4.5.2 The service plan involves the active participation of the participant and, when appropriate, other professionals and/or family members.

The first of these standards highlights the importance of treating the participant with dignity, as a unique individual. The second reaffirms the active involvement of the participant, because planning is not something done by the worker alone. In the language of Motivational Interviewing: "I'll help you solve this yourself!"

Reflection questions

1) To see if Figure 10.1: Planning for a Better Future tool (page 106) could be useful in working with participants, try it out for yourself. Think of one change you would like to make in some area of your life and apply this tool. After doing this, see if you are clearer about whether you want to proceed in this area.

2) In helping participants set goals, which of the SMART elements (Specific, Measurable, Attainable, Relevant, and Time-bound (pages 108-110) is most difficult for them?

CHAPTER 11

Achieving Goals and Maintaining Gains

This chapter discusses the interrelated work of helping participants reach goals they have set and hold on to the gains they have made. The phrase "choose, get, keep" (Anthony, et al., 1990) describes the process of planning (choose), goal attainment (get), and maintaining gains (keep). This highlights the importance of participants not stopping their work on issues once goals are initially met.

A reader might ask: "Why discuss goals in the previous chapter, action steps in this one?" Action steps are part of the work that happens after the initial planning and are often "works in progress." In case management, meeting with a participant weekly or every two weeks, the action steps may need to be modified as circumstances change.

In the previous chapter, it was stressed that goals need to be SMART goals. The same is true of action steps, the small accomplishments that lead to reaching the goal. These increments are also referred to as objectives or intermediate objectives. Depending on the nature of the action step, a number of tasks may be completed in accomplishing it.

When working with participants on formulating action steps, it is easy for the participant or worker to come up with one or two action steps that seem as if they should lead to goal completion. There are several limitations to immediately deciding on action steps. First, they may be too big. Think of the term "step" in the literal sense of a front-porch step. The step the worker and participant have identified may be the equivalent of a 38-inch step. When one large action step is broken down into smaller steps, they may seem more attainable.

Second, a limited number of possible action steps may signify that the worker and participant have not explored sufficient possibilities. The first ideas we have are not necessarily the best. The initial work of understanding the participant's situation and earlier planning with the participant may both be fruitful steps for generating potential action steps.

Third, workers can help participants see the completion of action steps as accomplishments and build on the success. Some participants come to us after a series of life events they often describe as personal failures. Their sense of efficacy or agency—the ability to achieve what is important to them—has been weakened by their life experiences. When these participants do accomplish tasks, their perception of their abilities and efficacy can begin to change. The worker can also use this success as a reference point as the participant works on other challenging tasks.

Finally, when a number of potential action steps have been identified, the worker and participant have the opportunity to decide which are most likely to be productive.

Strategies for identifying possible action steps

At times, the strategies or action steps to be taken may be clear and obvious. When that is not the case, the following approaches can be used to come up with possible steps:

Prompts

Open-ended questions, those that require more than a "yes" or "no" response or a few words, are useful in coming up with strategies for reaching goals. However, questions can be so open that participants may have trouble coming up with an answer. When a worker asks, "So, what can you do to reach the goal?" the participant may not know where to start. Egan (1994) suggests the use of prompts to narrow the questions to other people, programs, or organizations whose experience or resources are relevant to the participant's goals. These can include:

1) *People.* Who does the participant know who has done the kinds of

things the participant wants to accomplish, and how were things accomplished? What specific people could help the participant reach his/her goals?

2) *Communities or groups.* What groups or communities of people can help the participant reach his or her goals? Are there groups the participant would like to be a part of? Are there churches or other faith communities the participant would like to explore?

3) *Organizations or programs.* Are there programs out there that have helped others in similar situations? If the participant or worker does not know of the programs, how can they find out? (Egan, 1994; Locke, Garrison, and Winship, 1998).

Remembering what has worked before

In the midst of crisis, participants may not even remember what they have done well in the past. Questions can be used to help them name strategies that were useful in the past. Examples:

1) When you were confronted with this issue before, what did you do?

2) Which of these ways to deal with the issue were successful (at least for a while)?

3) What else have you found to be helpful?

Looking for resources in the participant's social network and social environment

In doing the assessment and in identifying possible action steps, it is likely that the worker will become aware of people in the participant's social network who are now or have been important to the participant. Potential resources other than former helpers—churches, social organizations, educational institutions, for example—may also have surfaced as a means to help participants reach goals or to support them in their efforts.

Workers can be alert for people and organizations in their social environment that may be a resource for their participants. In a small ecumenical program (three housing units) for homeless families, a part-time worker for the program also taught aerobics classes through the Recreation Department. More than once, she enlisted people from her aerobics classes to assist her participants (after checking with the participants first). The aerobics people were glad to be asked and provided assistance and support for her participants.

Providing information (carefully)

There may be information on resources or on approaches other individuals have used that the participant is not aware of. In asking the question "What have you tried?" the worker finds out that the participant indeed does not know of at least one potential resource.

The following ideas on effectively communicating new information are adapted from David Rosengren's *Building Motivational Interviewing Skills: A Participant Workbook:*

1) *Find out if the participant wants the information before offering it.* The worker may have information that could be useful to participants, but the worker needs to make sure participants want to hear it. One could ask, "I know of a resource that might be useful. Would you be interested in knowing about it?"
2) *Give a menu of options*—more than one potential resource. Providing more than one resource or strategy sends the message that we are not deciding what is best for the participant.
3) *When possible, provide information in the context of other participants.* When the worker presents information this way—"I know of others in situations similar to yours who have found this valuable"—participants tend to respond well to stories about what others like them have done (p. 223).
4) *Provide information in small chunks.* When the information is detailed and complicated, break down the information in small chunks, and check to make sure that each piece of information is understood before going on to the next (pp. 226-227). Providing the information also in written form makes it more understandable.

Difficulties in giving advice, necessity at times for providing direction

At times participants may say, "What should I do now?" or "What would you do if you were me?" Answering the questions directly can create problems. The worker may not know the participant's situation well enough to have an idea of what is most important to the participant—what is needed, what is possible. A separate issue arises when the worker offers advice on goals the participant accepts at face value. If things do not work out for the participant, the worker gets blamed.

Workers can respond to the question "What should I do now?" with questions to better understand the situation. One response is: "I don't think I know enough about what's going on to be much help. Tell me more about how..." Offering more than one option is another approach to answering the question. When the worker feels that in this situation not answering the question directly would be seen as evasive, the worker can share some aspects of his or her life to put the answer in context. A response from a worker might be, "What would I do if I were homeless now? Well, you need to understand that I'm 31 years old, and I've coped with my parents dying early and a divorce. I've figured out some things that work pretty well for me, but I have never had to deal with being homeless."

David Rosengren (2009) provides the following guidelines about advice giving:

1) *First ask permission.* The worker needs to make sure the participant is interested in what the worker has to say.
2) *Offer ideas.* The worker should not try to persuade or convince the participant.
3) *Be concise.* The worker should share the advice as directly and briefly as possible.
4) *Solicit what the participant thinks.* The worker should be sure the participant understands that she/he is free to disregard the worker's thoughts (pp. 230-31).

Understanding the Value of Potential Action Steps

The previous pages have discussed strategies the worker and participant can use to come up with potential action steps. Using prompts and remembering what has worked and when there have been exceptions to the problem can yield a number of potentially valuable action steps.

Should the worker attempt to persuade participants to consider or try things that are new or scary to the participant? It's a complicated issue, and workers need to keep in mind the value of self-determination. It is the participants' right to determine the form, direction, and substance of the help they receive (Rapp, 1998). Yet, before participants determine these, workers may want to help explore options they may not have considered. Most of us do not like to venture far from our "comfort zone," and participants are no exception.

In addition, many individuals with severe and persistent mental illness have developed survival skills that are contrary to the skills needed to achieve in the community. "Good" participants in mental health settings are those who are compliant in taking their medications and following treatment plans. However, compliant behaviors are rarely associated with achievement or growth that often involves some risks. Helping participants to unlearn behaviors no longer appropriate or to see things in new ways can be important.

Showing participants potential steps are possible

Individuals can be convinced, intellectually, that certain actions are worthwhile, but still may not be willing to try them. The fear of the new, low self-esteem, or a previous negative experience with something related to the potential action may all stand in the way of putting the plan into action. Individuals can learn new behaviors, and realize new behaviors are possible, by observing and/or imitating the behavior of another person (Bandura, 1969). Many times a step may involve a series of behaviors too complicated to explain, but that may be relatively easy to understand when observed or practiced.

Role playing can also be useful in specific situations such as simulating a job interview for a participant who gets nervous applying for jobs. Role playing provides an opportunity to apply and practice behaviors in a safe place before facing the challenge of using them in a new experience or a difficult situation.

Potential Action Step	Likelihood of Success	Impact On Reaching Goal
Scale: 1-10 (Ten is the highest score)		

Potential Action Steps Analysis

Figure 11.1

Deciding on Action Steps

Value of pencil and paper

Once a list of potential action steps has been compiled, the worker and participant will need to decide which to pursue. One tool the participant and worker can use is the Potential Action Steps Analysis shown above. After listing all potential action steps, the participant and worker can then estimate how likely the steps are to be achievable and, if achieved, how much this will contribute to reaching the goal. This information can then be factored into deciding which potential steps to pursue.

1. Based on the Potential Action Steps Analysis, which of the potential action steps appear to be good choices?
2. What other information about these possibly good choices increases or decreases their potential usefulness?

Implementing Action Steps

Turning plans into action steps usually requires connecting with resources, determining who is to do what and by what time, getting feedback on the process, and using that feedback for possible changes in the plan and also for learning.

Transforming potential resources into actual resources

As potential resources are identified, the worker and participant need to determine the availability, adequacy, accessibility, and accommodation of the resource (Kisthardt and Rapp, 1992). Resources that exist in the community may not have openings or may have requirements the participant does not meet. Transportation to the resource or its cost may present barriers to the resource being available to the participant. When the participant has mental health issues or other disabilities, it is important to consider how accommodating the resource will be.

Setting responsibility, monitoring progress, and providing positive feedback

Since one goal of the worker is that participants develop the skills for taking care of themselves, participants should assume or be given as much responsibility as possible. In the future, the participant can assume ongoing tasks for which the worker now is responsible. Too often in agencies, goals and objectives/action steps are established and then only referred to as part of the monitoring function, perhaps at quarterly meetings. Instead, reviewing the action steps can become a shared focus of every worker-participant meeting (Kisthardt, 1992, p. 79).

This ensures accountability and provides an opportunity to reflect on the process and to alter the plan when necessary. When the participant was not able to accomplish an agreed-upon task, reasons for this can be identified. It may be that the resource was not as appropriate or accessible as was thought. The participant's actions or inactions may be the main reason. The learning that occurred during an unsuccessful attempt can be valuable and used in revising action steps or approaches. If successful, the participant and worker are ready to move on to a new task related to the action step, a new action step, or a new goal (Rapp, 1998, p. 145).

Steps for maintaining effort and holding on to gains

If the goal of the participant is to change a behavior or pattern of actions, it may be difficult to tell from day to day or week to week if progress is being made. We are familiar with situations in which a worker sees a nephew or another child the worker hasn't seen for a while, and remarks to the parents on how much the child has grown. The parent may stop and say, "Well, I guess so!" The parent, who sees the child every day, is less aware of the changes because they are small.

So it is with participants who are changing behavior. When they can keep track of their behaviors, they are much more likely to stay on track in meeting goals. Support groups such as Alcoholics Anonymous, parenting groups, and Weight Watchers have realized success in tracking progress; group members also encourage others on small increments of progress.

The worker can use a few strategies to encourage participants and help them keep track of behaviors and progress. One of these is the use of _scaling questions_. Scaling questions (DeJong and Berg, 1998) can be used to get a rough idea about how things are going, and then to compare the responses from one time to another. For example, in a mentoring program with women working towards financial self-sufficiency, this would be an example of a scaling question: "On a scale of one to ten, with ten meaning you are doing very well, how good are you at managing your money?" At the beginning, the person might rate her money management skills as a "three." Two months later the worker may ask this question again, and the person says "five." In discussing what has changed, it can become clearer to the participant what she is doing better, and what she may need to do to be able to answer "seven" or "nine" to that question.

Another useful strategy may be to _keep track of success and what goes well in life_. Berg and Miller (1992) encourage participants to focus on the successful strategies they use instead of on troubling behaviors. Mothers who set a goal of yelling less at their children are encouraged to keep track of two things. One is the number of times they yell at their children every day. They may soon see there has been a 20 percent decline in yelling. This is not yet where the participant may want to be, but it is an indication of progress. The participant can also keep track of what she does when she overcomes the urge to yell. Paying attention to this, writing it down, and discussing it with the worker can accomplish several things. It allows the participant to discover which strategies work, and it gives the worker the opportunity to acknowledge the participant's insight and efforts. Both will contribute to goal achievement and maintenance.

Referrals

A Salvation Army corps, program, or service unit may not be able to offer all the services and resources participants need. One important role of the worker is that of linking the participant with needed formal or informal resources. It's more than just suggesting where someone can go to get help. To refer effectively one needs both a good knowledge of the community and also skills because:

1) The referral process often leads to the accomplishment of action steps. To determine which potential referral sources would be appropriate, the worker needs to be able to assess such factors as cultural background, resources, competencies, vulnerability, and commitment to change.
2) The worker needs to know the community resources and, when possible, be involved in staffing potential social services programs. This will help determine whether there would be a good fit between the participant's situation and potential resources.

Making an effective referral is often more difficult than it seems to a new worker. Just writing down the name and phone number of the referral source is often not enough. These tips were adapted from responses of 20+ Salvation Army workers at a 2013 workshop in Wisconsin on Connecting Clients with Resources:

1) Be accurate about the chances of getting help or support from other agencies. If participants are looking for assistance in paying back rent and the worker knows no other agency has funds left for this, make sure this is communicated.
2) Write out for the participants the necessary information regarding the resource (names, phone numbers, addresses, hours available, restrictions, requirements). It is important to provide the participants with the name of the specific contact person. Describe the resource contact person to the participants in terms of the worker's function as well as job title; personalize the contact person whenever possible.

3) If the worker is unsure that participants are able to fill out paperwork, the worker should have them do it in his or her office or do the paperwork with them.

4) Explore with the participants whether they want the worker to initially contact the resource or if they want to initiate contact. If participants prefer that the worker initiate the contact, it is preferable to do so in their presence. If the participants decide to contact the resource, it can sometimes be beneficial, with the participants' permission, for the worker to contact the referral source in advance.

5) Participants who are apprehensive may wish to be accompanied to the initial meeting with the resource contact person.

6) Remember that if participants are working with other agencies, the worker needs to get signed release forms so that he or she can communicate with these agencies.

7) Balancing "doing too much" and "doing too little" when connecting participants with services depends on the capabilities of the participants and the degree they are in crisis. If the participants are in crisis, the worker does a lot. If they are functioning well, the worker has the participants do as much of the work as possible. How much the worker does depends on the worker's relationship with the participants. The stronger the professional relationship, the easier it is to say "You need to do this" or "Let's do this together."

8) Follow-up is vital to ensure that the referral met the needs. The worker should ask the participants to let the worker know how the contact went after the initial meeting with the resource person.

9) In the process of trying to connect individuals with resources, make sure we are treating participants with dignity and honesty, that we are listening to them.

Reflection and learning

Both successful and unsuccessful participant activities provide the opportunity for positive feedback and for exploration of the strategies the participant used. When participants have been successful in doing something that was new for them, the worker can ask, "How did you manage that?" As a participant replies, the strategies he or she was using may become clearer. As participants "name and claim" the strategies they have successfully used, it becomes more likely they will use these again.

Many participants are not used to receiving positive feedback or praise. They may not have gotten much positive feedback on their talents or achievements as a child, in school, in relationships, or in the workplace. Accomplishments and partial accomplishments need to be named as they occur. The worker may pick up on small but important improvements in a participant's actions or attitudes towards reaching the goals. As these changes are pointed out, they are opportunities for small celebrations, for growth.

Maintaining Goal Achievement

In their work with participants with severe and persistent mental illness, Kisthardt and Rapp wrote, "Once a participant has achieved a desired end, the worker takes the position that much of the work is yet to be done" (1992, pp. 120-121). Many participants and former participants live on just enough money to get by, may live in communities where the supply of affordable housing is constantly shrinking, and/or may have ongoing mental health or substance abuse problems. For stability to be long-term, it is necessary to build in supports.

Challenging participants on goal attainment

Participants, like the rest of us, sometimes use only a fraction of their potential to deal with life issues and realize their dreams. It may be apparent to the worker that the participant's action or inaction interferes with attaining or maintaining a goal. The term "challenge" is used instead of the term "confront" to describe the worker's method in asking the participant to examine actions and thinking patterns that appear to be getting in the participant's way.

In order to effectively challenge participants, one needs to earn the right to challenge. Just as one can challenge good friends on their bad choices because of the relationship, some level of trust is essential in challenging a participant.

When does a worker challenge participants? In the following three areas accepting at face value the participant's words or assumptions would be counterproductive:

1) Failure to own problems and opportunities. If participants don't take responsibility for issues—"It's not my fault!"
2) Failure to state issues and situations as manageable or resolvable. Many people state issues using words such as "I can't do this" or "I'm not able to" or "I've never been able to."
3) Discrepancies and distortions in their version of events or reality. At times there is a discrepancy

between what a participant says and what he or she does. There also are instances when participants leave out important information or when their version of what happened is very different from that of others.

One can explore with participants the consequences of their proposed actions. A participant may be leaving a transitional housing program after a few weeks because "there are too many rules" and is going to live with a friend. The worker can ask her to look at what the possible consequences of her decision may be weeks and months down the road. People can also be challenged to examine how their actions are affecting others.

One can also challenge to action. Telling participants what to do is different from urging them to act, to make decisions, and to take some steps to change things.

Challenging participants is often more effective when the worker does it softly or tentatively. When a worker notices discrepancies or inertia, the worker does not accuse the participant, but "checks it out" with phrases such as:

1) "It seems to me that you're saying you want to do better and I still see you doing . . . ."

2) "Help me out with this. Your story of what happened is different from that of the boss at your previous job."

3) "When you say 'I can't do this,' it seems as if there's no possibility of things changing. Is that the way it is?" (material adapted from Egan, 1994; Locke, Garrison, and Winship, 1998).

When things are not working

At times, the work with participants goes well. There are also those situations when, after progress has been made and there is greater stability in the participant's life, things start to fall apart. In those cases, the worker can check to see what else is happening, determine if goals or aspirations have changed, reframe behaviors, identify a possible fear factor, and explore the consequences of behaviors.

Check to see what else is going on in their life

John Lennon is purported to have said, "Life is what happens to you while you're planning for the future." Many times crises arise in participants' lives—affecting them, or family, or friends—that take center stage and everything else gets put aside. Sometimes this is shared with workers; sometimes it is not. Missing appointments or not following through may happen because of a crisis.

Reframe missed appointments and tasks as another obstacle

Participants who see themselves as "messing up" may indulge in self-blame and reinforce the negative parts of their self-image. The worker can instead reframe the missing meetings or consequences of actions/inactions as another obstacle that will need to be overcome to reach the goals. Relationships may need to be mended, alternative steps identified. Moving out of the realm of self-blame and into planning can get things moving again.

Identify the possible role of fear in inaction

This may appear contradictory to the previous paragraph in which the worker was cautioned to stay away from self-blame. Some women experiencing homelessness "self-sabotage" when things are going well. They break a rule at a transitional housing program that will get them expelled. When asked why, one woman replied, "When things are going well, I'm just waiting for the other shoe to fall. I just decided to drop it myself." Exploring the fear, and helping participants learn to cope with the anxiety that comes with risk, may be essential.

Check if the changes in behavior and attitude are indications of need for disengagement with the worker

It may be that the participant has reached a place in his or her life in which less support is needed or the goal has become less important with changed circumstances. It may also be that the participant who has made progress has reached a "plateau" and may resume change efforts at another time.

Conclusion

Beyond maintenance—making continued progress.

The phrase "choose, get, keep" is in a way modest. It may reflect changes in the participant's life that match his/her aspirations, or it may just mean a family that was homeless is now housed, but precariously. Work with persons who are poor or who at the present or in the past have been homeless ideally should be more than helping people stay housed. As one advocate puts it, "We shouldn't be telling people we want them to just get by. The theme should be, 'Welcome to the party!'"

Reflection questions

1) On pages 118-120 are suggestions for coming up with action steps to help participants reach their goals. Which ones of these have you used? Are there other ways to come up with potential action steps not mentioned in these pages?

2) Effective ways of presenting new information and advice to participants is presented on pages 120, 121. How well does this information relate to any difficulties you have had in helping participants by providing new information or responding to requests for advice?

3) At times participants speak of their life and their challenges in ways that leave out important information or present a distorted view of their situation. How well does the material on challenging (pages 123, 124) give you approaches to use in those situations?

CHAPTER 12

Pastoral Care in The Salvation Army's Varied Settings

Chapter 2 discussed how the integration of faith, religion, and spirituality can promote positive outcomes in our social services ministries. Through our ability to provide this holistic approach, The Salvation Army is uniquely positioned to respond to the hurt and hopelessness we see in the eyes of people who come to our corps or social services units seeking help. The purpose of this chapter is to present ideas and tools that will aid workers and officers to approach spirituality in an ethical and missional manner.

Mission-driven ministry and teamwork

The Salvation Army's mission statement requires us to "preach the gospel of Jesus Christ," and "to meet human needs in His name without discrimination." To accomplish this, officers, workers, and the corps' congregations need to work together. Each group has different attributes and skills they can bring to the table. Together, as a team, our pastoral care ministry becomes stronger when challenges experienced by one group may not be visible to the others. Let's take a look at how each of these three groups can contribute to the pastoral care ministry.

The worker group, generally speaking, is most able to give their time to our participants. They often bring professional degrees, past experiences, and knowledge of their community's resources. Many workers feel their jobs are their personal ministry or calling. However, some workers are hesitant to wade into spiritual matters. "Research indicates that most practitioners have received little, if any, training on spirituality and religion during their graduate training. [Consistent with this lack of training...only 17 percent of NASW-affiliated direct practitioners felt that workers generally possessed the knowledge to address spiritual issues" (Hodge, 2006, p. 317). If the three groups are working as a team, this challenge could easily be addressed.

The workers will have the most intimate connection to the participant and should always be alert to signs that pastoral care might be needed. For example, the participant talks about loneliness and the lack of a social support system. This is a good time to mention the men's or women's fellowship of the corps. An example of this response is, "We have a lively women's friendship group here you might check out. They do some fun things and really enjoy their time together. Can I have somebody call you so that you can find out more about it?" A note to the Pastoral Care Representative (PCR) would also be appropriate, as loneliness is spiritual as well as social. Most often, the corps officer acts as the Pastoral Care Representative.

Always try to make the connection for the participant rather than just provide the information. It's very intimidating to come to a new place for the first time (especially a church). The worker can help pave the way for the participant by making a connection to someone in advance of a visit.

As the worker listens to the participant, other indications might be present that he/she could benefit from pastoral care: death in the family, life-changing decisions that are looming, questions about God, or other existential struggles. A proper response could be, "You have some really intense and deep things going on right now. Would you like to talk with someone who has more experience than me in dealing with tough issues like these? You know Jan; she actually has a background in talking with people about stuff like this. Can I ask her to give you a call?" If the participant seems unwilling, let it go and advise the PCR about what is going on. Then ask him/her to be hanging around after the next meeting, creating an opportunity for the participant to talk.

The officer group is able to bring

their knowledge from the Army's College for Officer Training and provide spiritual counseling to our participants. Through their roles as pastors and agency directors, officers are positioned to lead the pastoral care team. Because their appointments place heavy demands on their time, officers often find themselves in complicated dual relationships. Examples of these dual relationships include the corps soldier who also is receiving services through social services; or the worker who also is a corps soldier.

A strong team would help officers navigate these dual relationships and would support the officers' pastoral care efforts when they are pressed for time. Workers can perform spiritual assessments and arrange for participants and their officers to meet at a mutually agreeable time.

The heart of the helping process is *relationship;* therefore, pastoral care provided to social services participants must always be *relational.* To seek out and accept pastoral care from a corps officer or other PCR, a participant must know the:

1) PCR genuinely cares about *me* (the participant).
2) PCR is *happy* to make time to talk with me about my concerns or questions.
3) PCR knows me and my situation and will *understand* where I am coming from.
4) PCR is seen (by the participant) as one who has *credibility* as a spiritual and pastoral person.
5) PCR is a *trustworthy* person who will keep my confidence and not be judgmental.
6) The *corps* is a place filled with friendly people who value me; I feel safe and comfortable here.

Providing effective pastoral care for participants requires intentionality in building the relationship. The PCR must be present in the participant meeting space for that relationship to develop. Observing and experiencing faith in action by those who profess it often precedes developing an interest in Christian faith. A PCR whose approach to providing pastoral care is simply to expect participants to call for an appointment will fail to make this essential connection. Sometimes a corps soldier can act as a volunteer PCR.

It is important for the participant to meet the corps officers, who should be introduced as leaders and pastors: "Phyllis, I'd like you to meet Captain Jan Jenks. She and her husband are the pastors and leaders here." Like the PCR, officers should be visible and accessible during participant visits, making the extra effort to *go to the participant,* knowing the participant's name and building rapport over time.

To ask a participant to "call our corps officers and make an appointment for a spiritual assessment" is to create anxiety for the participant and a feeling of required compliance. By getting to know the participant over time, however, the officer can create an atmosphere in which the participant feels known and valued, and much of the pastoral care can take place on an informal basis (which is generally preferable). Once the relationship has been established, the worker could say to the participant, "Be sure to stop and say 'hi' to Captain Jan on your way out. She'll be disappointed if she doesn't get to see you today!" The officer could drop everything when the participant stops by, creating an opportunity to minister to the participant in an informal way.

The corps group can contribute to pastoral care on two levels. On the first level, soldiers volunteer themselves. Can they act as receptionists? Are they needed in the pantry? Sometimes our soldiers have skills they can teach our participants, such as cooking or budgeting. In a study of congregational volunteers in community-wide social services, long-term volunteers "reported that their volunteering was a response to their understanding or experience of God. Many participants talked of their volunteer activities as a response to 'a call'" (Garland, et al., 2009, p. 28). On the second level the corps group can contribute by having the corps be a full resource for our participants and their children. The corps congregation could become an important support system outside our community's social services organizations, providing support and stability.

The corps must be perceived by the participant as a safe and comfortable place in which there is a sense of being known and appreciated by those who "belong." It's important, especially in the beginning of a participant's journey, for the worker to make introductions to key individuals. This should be done in a casual way and not all at one time. For example, "Phyllis, this is Jan. She's around here a lot because she likes to talk with people who come in, so I'm sure you'll get to know her."

If "Jan" is the PCR, that doesn't need to be explained right away. If Jan is a corps member, then the introduction could include something about her role in the corps. "Jan is our young adult small group leader, and she likes to come down and hang out." If Jan is the corps officer, she can be introduced as "one of our pastors here at the Salvation Army church." Don't be in a hurry to get to your participant meeting, but allow a few minutes for Jan and Phyllis to chat a little. Jan will remember Phyllis' name and make a point of being around during your participant meetings so that she can continue to build a connection.

At an evaluation of one of the Central Territory's many shelters, a member of the evaluation team was tasked with interviewing an advisory council member. Through the course of the interview, the team member learned the man interviewed was a soldier at a local corps and a volunteer chaplain for the city's fire department. Near the close of the interview, the team member asked if he could get the council member's opinion, as a chaplain, on how to address some emerging trends that threaten effective pastoral care. He went on to share his frustrations and observations around this issue. When done, the advisory council member replied with one word: "Communication." Feeling the answer to be too simple, the evaluator expanded on his previous explanation with even more examples of challenges preventing good pastoral care. Again, the advisory council member responded with one word: "Communication."

All hands on deck

Pathway of Hope training and implementation planning stress the importance of an "All hands on deck" approach that reflects the involvement of the corps officer(s), social services staff, and the corps' soldiery in intentional interaction to holistically serve our participants. The pilot site in Green Bay, Wisconsin, seemed to grasp this concept when the initial training manual for the Pathway of Hope was being drafted. At that time, Captain Katherine Clausell was the corps officer at Green Bay. And she was asked to articulate how she understood the "All hands on deck" approach worked at her appointment. This is what she had to say:

> Recognizing that corps officers and social services staff have many demands for their time and attention, a shared " all hands on deck" approach to developing and implementing the Pathway of Hope initiative is absolutely essential for its success. Central to an "all hands on deck" approach is the intentional integration of case management staff [workers], corps officers, pastoral care representatives, appropriate corps soldiery, and community stakeholders (volunteers and Advisory Board and Auxiliary members).

The worker's responsibility is to coordinate the participants' action plans and lead the Army's relationship with their families. The worker should introduce the corps officer or Pastoral Care Representative to the participants very early in their involvement in the Pathway of Hope process. The Pastoral Care representative will conduct a spiritual assessment, assisting participants with their spiritual needs as requested. Connecting participants with resources within the corps and referring corps to this shared approached will ensure that participants interact with the social services staff assisting them. Also, the entire corps leadership positions themselves to help Pathway of Hope participants break the cycle of crisis and vulnerability. This approach will help us achieve our goal of bridging participants to our corps' congregation, leaving participants with an enduring impression of the corps ministry work we do. With the expectation of frequent participant contact (at least initially), participants may benefit from meeting with others beside their assigned worker to help them attain their action plan's goals.

If the corps staff and Pathway of Hope participants can see they have a network of people and services to help them along the path out of poverty, no one entity will feel as if it bears the weight of the family's success alone. We are not suggesting that every time Pathway of Hope participants arrive for their appointment they are greeted by the entire team; rather, participants should be able to count upon any team member to be actively engaged and ready to partner with them as they progress along their own "pathway."

A number of people in the corps building should carry out this same intentionality of knowing the participant—the corps officers, other workers, receptionists, food pantry workers, and key volunteers. When the participant comes to his/her meetings with positive anticipation and a feeling "these people know me, like me, believe in me, and are on my side," a powerful impact can be produced. Confidentiality prevents everyone from knowing details about the participant's situation and goals, but everyone can certainly affirm faithfulness to the process and create a welcoming environment.

The Salvation Army National Social Services Standards

In 2009, the Commissioners Conference approved the first Salvation Army National Social Services Standards Manual. The Western Territory was charged to lead the tool's development, with strong collaboration with the Central Territory. The two territories reached out to over 100 Salvation Army officers and staff members from the Army's four U.S. territories and the Canada & Bermuda Territory to develop a manual that is relevant, comprehensive, user-friendly, and beneficial to all social services programs. This standard development process included careful examination of existing accreditation bodies such as Council on Accreditation (COA), Child Welfare League, Commission on Accreditation of Rehabilitation Facilities (CARF), Joint Commission (formerly Joint Commission on Accreditation of Health Care Organizations (JCAHO) and others. In addition, the co-authors of the manual reviewed and incorporated many existing social services standards of the Central, Canada, and Bermuda territories

In 2013, The Salvation Army National Social Services Standards Manual, 2nd edition, was approved by the Commissioners' Conference. This revision, led by the Central Territory with support from the Western Territory, resulted in a more targeted, streamlined, and effective evaluation process. The National Social Services Standards include critical program benchmarks in eight key areas: 1) Organization, Governance, and Administration, 2) Community, 3) Personnel, 4) Service, 5) Pastoral Care, 6) Finance & Contract Management, 7) Facility & Equipment, and 8) Safety and Risk Management. Because this chapter is about providing pastoral care, it is important to understand the following chapter in the Army's National Social Services Standards:

National Social Services Standards Pastoral Care Chapter

"The provision of pastoral care in all Salvation Army service is central to our Christian mission and intentionality is paramount when providing pastoral care. Many of our participants are aware of our Christian motivation, but we cannot rely totally on them to initiate a spiritual conversation. That is why the pastoral care chapter calls for the program to have a written pastoral care plan. According to the standards, pastoral care includes:

a. Providing spiritual care and ministry to participants, volunteers, staff, and community residents as appropriate.

b. Developing relationships of trust.

c. Providing opportunities to worship.

d. Connecting participants to opportunities for further spiritual development.

All stakeholders, including the corps officer(s), workers, and members of the corps should be involved in developing the pastoral care plan. Furthermore, the pastoral care plan should be reviewed and revised annually and with a change of officer appointment." A sample pastoral care plan is included as Appendix C (p. 228.)

The next section of the pastoral care chapter considers how the pastoral care plan will be carried out and who is responsible.

The standards call for a designated Pastoral Care Representative (PCR). This position does not always need to default to the corps officer; however, the designated individual needs to be qualified by virtue of education and/or experience to meet the demands of this position. The role and responsibilities of the PCR are to be clearly defined in a position description of those duties (Appendix D). A PCR needs to have a reasonable workload that allows the person to effectively carry out his or her responsibilities. This includes (but is not limited to):

1) Provision of religious services (i.e., worship services, funerals, weddings, character-building programs, etc.).
2) Visitation.
3) Bible studies.
4) Staff support.
5) Crisis support.
6) Referral sources to other denominations or faiths.
7) Facilitating/coordinating faith group involvement in pastoral care.
8) Making Christian literature available.
9) Spiritual counseling and prayer.
10) Performing spiritual assessments.
11) Other outreach as appropriate to the program type.

The Salvation Army is positioned to address many of our participants' basic needs. A strength of the Army is our ability to attend to their spiritual needs. In the assessment phase of the case management process, workers often use different assessment tools to learn about the strengths of the participants and the challenges they face. During that time, a spiritual assessment also should be made. A Spiritual Assessment is a tool PCRs can use to guide their conversation with a participant and gather information about a participant's spirituality (Appendix E).

A decision about who conducts the spiritual assessment is a critical part of the pastoral care plan. Having the PCR conduct the spiritual assessment is a great way to help build rapport with the participant. In fact, some divisions in the Central Territory have policies that call for the PCR always to be the person to administer the spiritual assessment. Therefore, the general practice seems to be that the PCR completes the assessment during a *pastoral care meeting,* but this does not have to be the case. Completion may depend on program type, staffing levels, and the PCR's availability.

When the PCR is unable to conduct spiritual assessments, workers should be familiar enough with the Spiritual Assessment to capture key information that comes up naturally during their participant meetings. For example, the participant mentions that St. Andrew Church has been helping him or her with food. "That's been a big help, I'm sure. How did you get connected to St. Andrew? "the worker asks. Information might flow that the participant's children are part of the youth group and that the entire family is grounded in their Catholic faith. The worker can then help connect the participant with the PCR and be able to give the PCR some good background information to start with.

Relational ministry is a key component of successful pastoral care implementations. That is why the pastoral care chapter calls for the PCR to have the opportunity through his/her efforts to interact with participants. The PCR should have a consistent scheduled time when he/she is available and near the worker's office. This creates the connection that makes it possible for the participant to want and receive pastoral care. The PCR should assume there will be participants wanting to talk and should prepare a designated quiet space. There impromptu conversations can take place without interruption or fear of being overheard.

It is important that pastoral care be offered without any pressure and that care be given to avoid even the appearance of coercion. Participants should be assured their involvement with pastoral care or lack of it does not affect other services they are receiving through any Salvation Army program. Lastly, federal and/or state money should not be used to pay for the PCR or any PCR activities.

An earlier section of this chapter addressed how successful pastoral care implementations involve teamwork. The pastoral care standards indicate that whenever our programs provide workers, the PCR needs to have regular communication with the program staff regarding the care of the participants. One way to accomplish this is to include the PCR in clinical case review meetings. Here the team of workers reviews each participant's progress, discusses challenges they are having, and receives support and guidance from their supervisor and each other.

Being a worker with The Salvation Army can be emotionally demanding, and our staff and volunteers may at times need spiritual support for a variety of reasons. The PCR should establish an approachable presence with the program's staff and volunteers. Also, devotions and prayer may be a regular part of staff meetings, and opportunities for the PCR to encourage and come alongside the staff should be intentionally sought.

The corps can play a significant role in the experience participants have with The Salvation Army. Much of the success in coordinating with corps depends on how prepared the corps are to accept participants into their church environment. In 2004, the Army's Central Territory surveyed 23 officers who had been identified by their Divisional Social Services Directors and Divisional Commanders as being able to successfully bridge participants to their corps. Through the survey it became evident that successful corps were deliberate, their congregation saw newcomers as an opportunity for growth, and the corps officer played a critical role. The corps congregation should be prepared spiritually and emotionally to accept participants into the church home prior to implementing any bridging initiative. Participants who are unfamiliar with attending church should have the norms of church participation (dress, mobile phone usage, sleeping, etc.) explained to them prior to attending a corps worship service.

Frequently, through the intervention of one of our programs, a participant's faith is renewed, and they desire to return to the church or denomination they left. The PCR is to assist participants in finding or reconnecting with their church home. If a participant practices another faith, the PCR should be able to refer them to a faith community of their choice. To accomplish this, the PCR should create a referral network of area churches and faith communities.

The last section of the pastoral care chapter refers to documentation. It is recommended that some documentation be kept. A copy of the participant's spiritual assessment should be included in his/her case file. Pastoral care meetings should be noted in the participant's case file's progress notes under the heading "Pastoral Care Note." The purpose of the notation is to communicate to the worker that the PCR had an interaction with the participant. Therefore, the note can be generic in nature. This pastoral care note is helpful when working as a clinical team. PCRs should maintain their documentation and session notes in a locked file drawer in their office.

Conclusion

Touching the lives of people creates opportunities for spiritual ministry.

The most effective pastoral care plan is a relationship-building plan that connects the participant to as many people as possible in the corps. When the participant feels known, safe, and valued, he/she will be more open to the spiritual ministry at the heart of all we do. In the business world there is a principle known as "managing by walking around." In social services and in our corps, let's "minister by walking around." Touching the lives of people and demonstrating the love of Christ creates opportunities for spiritual ministry and requires us to go where the people are. Often, the most powerful pastoral care doesn't happen in an office by appointment. It happens by divine appointment when we are willing to put aside our "busy-ness." We care when we are present and reach out to people who desperately need to experience the love of Christ flowing through His servants.

Reflection questions

1) Think of a time when the workers, officer(s), or pastoral care representative and the corps have practiced the "All hands on deck" approach. Can you identify any key elements or highlights of your efforts that could be replicated by your team with your current caseload?

2) Do you have a pastoral care plan? If you were to create or revise your current plan, who are the key players you should seek input from?

3) To what degree is your pastoral care plan built around your team's strengths?

4) On a scale of one to ten, how would you rate your comfort level in addressing a participant's spirituality? Is there a point during a spiritual assessment or discussion when your comfort level increases?

5) To what degree does your corps demonstrate a welcoming spirit and show acceptance to participants when they attend a corps service or activity? What could be done to help participants feel more welcomed in your corps?

CHAPTER 13

Understanding Communities and Community Collaboration

To work effectively in a community, it is necessary to understand the community and to know how to collaborate with other organizations and individuals in that community. As stated in *The Salvation Army National Social Services Standards Manual,* programs serve clearly defined target communities. Therefore, there needs to be ongoing efforts to understand the ethnic, cultural, and socioeconomic makeup of each target community. Two lenses through which to view a community are 1) examining the contexts of a community and 2) assessing the resources within a community. Also, to serve those in need in a community, effective collaboration is essential.

Contexts of a community*

Understanding the context of a locality includes assessing the impact of national and international factors as well as technological changes. What happens in global financial markets can impact a small town in Michigan and a city in Oregon. On a more local level, having a thorough understanding of the locality is necessary to provide leadership for sustainable change and to effectively practice in that community. In this section, the important elements of

* This section is adapted with permission from Winship, James (2014b). Community Context. Unpublished manuscript.

the community context will be discussed as well as issues related to understanding specific groups of people, especially minority communities.

Economic factors affecting local communities

The United States has recovered somewhat from the Great Recession of 2008, yet economic challenges in recent decades have intensified. The number of middle-class jobs is declining, and inequality is rising, with the richest 400 Americans having a combined net worth greater than the bottom 60% of Americans (Krueger, 2012).

One impact of the shrinking income of Americans at the middle and low end of the economic ladder is revealed in a study by the Schwartz Center for Economic Policy Analysis at the New School. According to the analysis, 34.6 percent of workers aged 45-54 and 31.2 percent of the workforce aged 55-64 are projected to live at or below 200% of the poverty level when they retire (Klingensmith, 2014).

The data presented above is national, and the economic well-being of communities varies greatly. Answering the following questions can help workers understand the specifics of the economic situation in their community.

1) What are the major sources of employment in the community? Are there jobs that are well-paid and family-supporting, as well as jobs that pay $12 an hour or less?
2) What is the unemployment rate? How does this compare to other nearby communities or to state/national rates?
3) Are there reasons for young people to stay in the community as they reach adulthood or for other people to move into this community?
4) In the school district, what percentage of students receives free or reduced lunches?
5) How big is the donor base when money needs to be raised for charitable causes?

Geography, natural environment, and demography

By looking at any community on a map, workers can ascertain important information. If it is a city or small town, are there Interstate or other four-lane highways that make it easy for people and manufactured goods to get to and from the community? Also, look at how the city or small town is situated on a map or on Google Earth. Are there important geographical features? These can include mountains that make it more time-consuming for travel or include areas of scenic beauty that could increase tourism (and with high tourism, affordable housing may be a concern for local residents).

Through reviewing census documents (www.census.gov), one can determine the demographic makeup of a community by age, race and ethnicity, economical levels, etc. Examine the changes in these over ten-year periods—from 1990 to 2000, from 2000 to 2010—to understand the demographic changes in the county or locality.

The following questions can help workers understand a community's geography, natural environment, and demography:

1) How isolated is the locality and neighborhoods within the community? For localities, are there four-lane highways that connect it to other places? For neighborhoods and within counties, are there ways to get to other places in the city/county?
2) To what degree is the weather an overall advantage or disadvantage to the community? Is the community vulnerable to severe weather—flooding, tornadoes, or earthquakes? How dependent on the weather is the local economy—for example, in farming communities?
3) What is the demographic makeup of the community, especially racial/ethnic, and age ranges? How has that changed in recent decades?

History, traditions, and culture

Each community has its unique history. Understanding what life was like before a worker started to serve in that community—years, decades, or even longer ago—can help the worker understand current practices. For example, Wisconsin has the dubious honor of leading the nation in binge drinking and percentage of drinkers in the population. The heavy drinking in the state can relate to cultural heritage, with 43 percent of the state's inhabitants tracing their ancestry to stein-heisting Germany (Rommell, 2014).

The following questions can help workers understand the impact of the history, traditions, and culture of a community:

1) What percentage (more or less) of the residents have lived there all their lives? What percentage is from families who have lived there for more than one (or two or three) generations?
2) What ethnic groups settled the region/area/community, and how do the values of those groups

now affect values, culture, and what is accepted and acceptable behavior?

3) What are people in this community proud of?

4) How important is education to residents? How important is having recreation programs and other services?

Social structures

A community's health can be measured by the degree to which existing social structures and organizations provide opportunities for people to be involved with others, and in some cases provide service to others. It has been documented that there are fewer social structures in communities now as compared to the past (Putnam, 2000), but this varies greatly from community to community. The following questions can help workers understand the social structures of a community:

1) What churches are there in the community? How important are these to the community? Do they provide any help to nonmembers?

2) What service organizations (Kiwanis, Optimist, Rotary, etc.) are there in the community? What needs do they meet or support?

3) What groups of people do not appear to have social structures available that meet their needs or wants?

Political structure and climate

City and county governments make decisions that affect low-income residents and the level of health, recreation, and social services in an area. The following questions can help workers understand the political structure and climate:

1) For city/county government, how much representation is there by districts instead of city/county-wide?

2) How involved are citizens in committees and advisory boards in the city/county?

3) Are there groups or individuals that appear to have much influence on the decisions of the city/county?

Understanding specific minority communities in your locale

In localities in which The Salvation Army serves sizable minority communities, it is essential that those providing social services be knowledgeable about them. What are the communities' strengths and the issues facing those communities? Do they work with grassroots groups and key leaders in those communities?

A starting place is to understand the

demographic realities of the specific service area, knowing informally which ethnic, racial, or cultural minorities live in the service area and how large each group is. It is also essential to be knowledgeable about the informal social supports and natural helpers a minority population may use. The religious leaders of the community (ministers in black churches, a priest who delivers the mass in Spanish at a Catholic church, a Buddhist monk) are natural contacts for The Salvation Army to cultivate.

The Salvation Army can reach out to and become involved in decision making by serving on advisory boards, committees, etc. It also is valuable to connect with important groups and individuals in minority populations—ministers/religious leaders, advocacy groups, and tribal or cultural organizations. Workers can also participate on committees or task forces led by agencies already providing culturally specific services, such as the National Refugee Association, Hispanic Alliance, and the Urban League.

Our understanding of minority communities can lead to a greater focus in our services on ethnic strengths and strongly held values. If the corps is providing congregate meal sites in neighborhoods with high numbers of poor individuals from an ethnic minority group, it can be wise to work with people in that community to serve foods people prefer to eat. Programs for family support in Latino neighborhoods can start by recognizing the commonly held desire for intact, strong families, then developing ways to strengthen the bonds between couples and between parents and children.

Understanding the resources in your community*

Communities have four broad types of resources that can be used in Salvation Army programing to meet participants' needs. These are:

Programs, such as rent and utility assistance, food and meal programs, affordable or free health care, legal assistance, mental health and substance abuse programs, and housing/shelter.

People, including volunteers, those individuals with special expertise or individuals whose endorsement carries weight in the broad community or within specific groups.

---

*Material in this section has been adapted from The Pathway of Hope Training Manual, The Salvation Army Central Territory, (2012) Des Plaines, IL.

Funding, including federal/state/ local funding, United Way, and/or community foundations, donations from community service groups or individuals.

In-kind resources, including food and other supplies, the availability of free meeting or activity space, and transportation.

The Pathway of Hope Training Manual provides the following information on community resource strategies:

1) *Strengthen existing relationships*—Strengthen the Army's existing relationships with individuals, organizations, and other coalitions.
Example: Your corps has an existing relationship with a food pantry and has deepened your relationship with it to provide nutrition classes.

2) *Tap potential resources*—Tap into underutilized resources the Army doesn't currently provide or access.
Example: Your corps joins a coalition of social services providers working to alleviate poverty through government assistance; there is a workplace development agency workers have not used for participant referrals.

3) *Create new programs or resources*—Create new programs or resources in collaboration with other influential groups or organizations.
Example: Your corps hosts a job fair, connecting participants to prospective employers and Salvation Army corporate partners.

4) *Do nothing*—Given other priorities, timing, funding needs, or mission alignment, it does not make sense for your corps to undertake certain activities at the time.
Example: There is a lack of adequate child care in your community. Look for other organizations that could take this on before deciding whether this is the most important new program to launch.

Effective community collaboration

Collaborative efforts may arise out of mandates that require organizations to cooperate in order to receive funding. They also may be the result of trust developed over time between service providers and groups in a community. Models and best practices in collaboration have been developed that can lead to the creation of shared goals, enhanced relationships, and alignment and operational coordination of initiatives within communities*:

*Material in this section has been adapted from The Pathway of Hope Training Manual, The Salvation Army Central Territory, (2012) Des Plaines, IL.

1) *Joint partnership with affiliated programing*—Two or more organizations join their operations for programing or delivery of services.
Example: In Boulder, Colorado, four organizations that each had been soliciting school supplies for children in low-income families formed a joint program "Crayons to Calculators." This met the need without gaps or duplication of efforts.

2) *Joint partnership for issue advocacy*—Organizations join forces to share their collective message with one voice.
Example: The Center to Prevent Childhood Obesity (run by the Robert Wood Johnson Foundation) is a collaboration of local, state, and national researchers, advocates, and other partners who are promoting strategies to prevent childhood obesity through policy and community change.

3) *Shared administration or program operations*—Organizations achieved efficiencies by sharing administrative and/or program support.
Example: People Assisting the Homeless (PATH) in Los Angeles provides a single-site service center for 20 social services providers working towards common housing support goals. Through administrative support (e.g., finances, HR, PR), PATH's partners benefit from reduced costs and greater coordination of processes and protocols.

4) *Shared outcomes and databases*—Organizations work together to achieve shared, co-created outcomes and collectively track their progress against those shared outcomes.
Example: The STRIVE initiative is made up of 300 education-related organizations in the Cincinnati/Northern Kentucky region. These groups are organized into fifteen networks by type of intervention. Each network meets biweekly to share information, develop common outcomes, collaboratively problem solve, and coordinate efforts. These efforts are supported by strong data systems and technology.

Obstacles to working together

For a number of reasons, agencies do not work together effectively. One has to do with the relationships that helping organizations and agencies have by design. Often the best relationships are between organizations whose services do not overlap, but benefit the same kinds of participants. For example, in a community The Salvation Army provides emergency shelter, but another agency offers first month's rent assistance to the shelter residents.

There also are situations in which other organizations are doing many of the same things The Salvation Army is doing in a city—food bank or food vouchers, housing assistance, etc. Although there is not direct competition in this instance, both organizations may be searching for volunteers and sources of support from the same churches and civic organizations and are serving similar populations.

The nature of the organizations themselves also contributes to the lack of contact and cooperation between agencies serving similar participants in a community. An example would be a situation in a mid-sized city in which individuals seeking to leave public assistance and enter the workforce may be working with a public welfare agency, with a for-profit agency with a contract to move welfare recipients into work situations, and with The Salvation Army. Workers in all three organizations may be suspicious of the work and motives of the other organizations.

Workers at The Salvation Army may see the welfare department workers as rule-bound bureaucrats, only concerned with following procedures and not caring about whether the family's needs are met. The workers at the for-profit job center can be seen as only wanting to get people into a job and keep them there for ninety days. Those are the performance measures on which that agency will be judged. Workers at the other two agencies may view the workers at the Army as evangelistic do-gooders who do not deliver a tangible product.

Negative views of other agencies can be reinforced by the accounts of participants with whom Army staff have contact. When staff hear from participants about insensitive, punitive workers at another agency, when they do not have much direct contact with workers at that agency, nor direct knowledge of the agency's policies and mission, it is quite natural to assume the worst. When participants complain of their treatment at another agency, it may be that they were treated unfairly. It may also be that the worker was simply following agency policies and procedures and had no other options.

Workers tend to have negative opinions of personnel at other helping organizations when their only contact with them is adversarial—when one telephones to find out why some services weren't provided, or calls a Salvation Army worker essentially to tell that worker how to do his/her job.

In a study of relations between a welfare department and other organizations in Michigan, the author found that most of the minimal contact frontline workers at the welfare department had with social workers from private agencies occurred when the workers conducted participant advocacy. They would inquire as to why a certain action was not taken, why authorization was so slow, or why additional verification was required.

From the point of view of the welfare workers, they were following their procedures (and the law). When they were confronted by workers at other agencies, those experiences confirmed that other agencies did not understand their mandates or services. This tended to further increase the isolation of the welfare department workers (Sandfort, 1999).

The importance of informal communication

Regardless of the degree of formal collaboration within a community, informal communication between workers at different organizations is invaluable. If there is an opportunity to meet other workers at community-wide training events or at meetings of local human service coalitions, several helpful things can occur. First, staff can learn more about what is done at other agencies. There's a saying that things work best when all are "singing from the same page of the hymnbook." That's ideal, and the next best thing is to at least understand the "hymnbook" of other agencies.

Second, it is important to get to know the workers at social services agencies as individuals. Then, when there is a need to talk to that worker about a referral or a participant complaint, the conversation is with someone already known, at least minimally, with whom there perhaps may be rapport.

Conclusion

We need to understand our communities.

Just as it is important to individualize participants, realizing no two are alike, we also need to be conscious of the unique characteristics and assets as well as the difficulties of a community in which we work. We need to understand our communities as well as we can, get to know community partners, and find ways to work together for the benefit of the people we serve and the well-being of the community.

Reflection questions

1) When you consider the community you work in, are there ways you can build on the history, traditions, culture, and/or social structures (pages 141, 142) in strengthening the services of your program/corps?

2) On pages 143, 144 four kinds of resources are discussed—programs, people, funding, and in-kind resources. In your community is there one or more of these your corps/program could develop further?

CHAPTER 14

Social Justice and Advocacy

In the section on Responsibility to Society in The Salvation Army Social Services Code of Ethics (Appendix A) is the statement: "Salvation Army personnel will promote social justice and the general well-being of the community and advocate for policies and programs that ensure all persons have access to human resources."

Social Justice

The Salvation Army's commitment to social advocacy for social justice dates back to its earliest years. In 1885, Bramwell Booth, the oldest son of the founder William Booth, was in organizational charge of The Salvation Army. When a girl came to the Army's London headquarters with a story of escaping the night before from a prostitution house where she had been taken essentially into slavery, Booth prodded a journalist to investigate the situation. An international trade in teenage girls was discovered, one that included drugging girls and sending them in nailed coffins to special-order participants. Salvation Army soldiers collected 393,000 signatures and presented them to Parliament. As a result of their efforts, a bill was passed in 1885 raising the age of consent to sixteen and virtually stopping the intercontinental traffic in girls.

The Salvation Army's role in systemic advocacy for social justice was clearly expressed by Lt. Colonel

Paul E. Bollwahn, former National Social Services Secretary:

The Salvation Army Social Mandate

Our mission requires us to do all we can to "meet human needs" according to the gospel. Such is predicated on the place and time of our beginnings. Our heritage requires that we continue to serve in the context of our niche. Therefore, today we are indeed "up to our eyeballs" rendering a continuum of services because we serve in the context of:

1) Psalm 82:3 (KJV): "Defend the poor and fatherless: do justice to the afflicted and needy," based on the assumption of Psalm 12:5 that God Himself defends the oppressed, the poor, and the needy.
2) Proverbs 31:9 (LB): "Speak up for the poor and helpless and see that they get justice."
3) John 4:4 (LB): "[Jesus] had to go through Samaria" to meet the spiritual and social needs of a despised Samaritan woman. His advocacy elevated those despised and second-class people to equality with those already affirmed by society.
3) Luke 4: 18-19 (NKJV): "The spirit of the Lord is upon Me, because He has anointed Me to preach the gospel to the poor . . . to set at liberty those who are oppressed." As Jesus preached in the synagogue with this allusion to the Old Testament Jubilee Year that liberated the obligations of the poor, He proclaimed a greater liberation. He used this quote from Isaiah to announce His ministry, describing six aspects of it—one of which was advocacy for the poor and oppressed.
5) Ephesians 4:11-13 (NIV): "So Christ himself gave the apostles, the prophets, the evangelists, the pastors and teachers, to equip his people for works of service, so that the body of Christ may be built up. "
6) Matthew 25: 40, 45 (J.B. Phillips) "I assure you that whatever you did for the humblest of my brothers you did for me. . . I assure you that whatever you failed to do for the humblest of my brothers you failed to do for me."

These scriptures mandate the church's involvement with the poor. Our mission is based on our perspective in theology. From the Wesleyan tradition we believe that spiritually dead and separated humankind is awakened through prevenient* grace to the realization that God made a plan of redemption and invites their appropriation of it in faith. Through prevenient grace, universally given, freedom of choice, responsibility, and worthiness of personhood are restored in the individual.

More than a century after The Salvation Army's leading role in legislation on human trafficking, the

Army in the United States and abroad is an integral part of a movement for the abolition of sex trafficking and other forms of commercial sexual exploitation.

Advocacy

Advocacy efforts can be divided into *systemic advocacy:* addressing policies or decisions in the community, state, or nation that disadvantage or are oppressive to groups of people, and *participant advocacy:* helping those we serve to obtain the provisions and fairness to which they are entitled. Because frontline social services staff will be more involved in participant advocacy, this is the central focus of this chapter.

Techniques for participant advocacy

Before initiating an advocacy effort, it is important to fully understand the situation. There may be times when a person seeking emergency assistance from The Salvation Army explains that she was denied assistance somewhere else, even though she knows she met the requirements for the assistance. It may be that she was unjustly denied services or benefits, or there may be other reasons for the service denial. Before proceeding to advocate for the participant, it is wise to:

1) Understand the range of services offered and the policies of the agency in question. When workers investigate this, they may discover that the person who was denied services is not eligible for those services, or the agency did not have the legal authority to grant the benefits or services. The workers may also find that the person is eligible for the services.
2) Learn the appeal process of the agency, so that the worker will be guiding the participant in ways that can lead to resolution of the issue. Understanding any legal aspects of the appeal process is also important.
3) With the participant's permission, check with the staff at the organization where there is a concern to see if the participant has given the complete story. It may be that the participant thought she was not eligible unless she brought in an address verification, and she only heard the part about not being eligible. Of course, the worker needs to get informed consent from the participant be-

*A theological concept—the concept of God that precedes repentance and conversion and predisposes the heart to seek God prior to any initiative on the part of the recipient. Therefore, through grace, people choose to be saved and nurtured in a restored righteousness. They are not subject to a predetermined selection of God. All people are deserving through Christ's supreme sacrifice.

fore proceeding.

4) Make sure participants have given permission to proceed with the advocacy and are aware of possible consequences or repercussions if the worker continues.

When the participant and worker decide advocacy is necessary, and the worker is advocating with a staff member from another agency, it is essential to communicate respect for the other staff member. It is easy to personalize a situation or see another agency as the enemy. Workers need to guard against self-righteousness or righteous indignation. The goal is to help participant(s), not shame a worker or agency.

It is essential to communicate the participant's position and the desired goal of the advocacy. As that staff member responds, the Salvation Army worker needs to be actively listening for clear understanding, for possible useful information, and for possible courses of resolution. Techniques for successful participant advocacy can include:

1) Providing the opportunity for the staff person from the other agency to come up with a solution or suggest one that saves face for the agency.

2) Finding out how much discretion workers have by asking if there have been times when an exception similar to this one has been granted. The worker may also be able to find out this information by learning of practices of similar organizations in other areas.

3) Demonstrating the exception by showing the uniqueness of this participant's situation and how it deserves the broadest interpretation of the rules.

4) Insisting on common sense by showing how a common- sense approach supports the participant's position, even if there are technicalities in regulations that might be used against this position.

5) Asking to see the policies when participants have been refused service because they do not fit the requirements of agency policy or the law. If the worker is not sure the participants are not eligible, ask to see the policy or law. If a law or an administrative rule is at issue, find out what the law is and bring a copy to the meeting.

6) Asking to see a supervisor if there is not an acceptable resolution to the situation, as it may very well be that the worker does not have discretion in this area, while a supervisor might.

Whenever possible, it is important

to advocate *with* participants, instead of advocating *for* them. People develop a sense of their own competence and power when they advocate for themselves. Successful legal or other advocacy may make real improvements in people's lives. However, if the participants are not involved in the advocacy efforts, the relationship of power may not be changed between these institutions and the people served by them (Locke, Garrison, and Winship, 1998).

Conclusion

Systemic changes may be needed.

At times advocacy on a scale larger than helping individual participants may be needed. Three instances when advocacy on a larger scale may be warranted are: 1) a number of people in similar circumstances are not being given services or opportunities for which they qualify; 2) services provided are not accessible or helpful to participants; 3) services provided do not treat participants with dignity.

However, if those circumstances arise, one's supervisor and the corps officers (or a level higher) should be alerted to the situation. They would decide if any action should be taken.

Reflection questions

1) When you think about the life situation of participants with whom you work, do you consider areas in which The Salvation Army could work for social justice on the national level, as William Booth and Bramwell Booth did in the 1800s in England?

2) In Chapter 13, Understanding Communities and Community Collaboration, the need for forming relationships with other service providers was discussed. There are times when Salvation Army workers need to advocate on behalf of participants with these service providers. Have you been able to do effective participant advocacy while still maintaining a working relationship with the service provider in these situations?

PART IV

How to Effectively Use Faith in Action

CHAPTER 15

Case Studies: Faith in Action

When we work with those coming for assistance for material or other needs, we are part of The Salvation Army's more than 150 year-old ministry to the whole person.

At times, what we do contributes to transformations in people's lives. The following are "success stories" of the Central Territory in 2014:

Deasia was 13 when her mother contacted our office in Englewood seeking help for her daughter. She needed assistance due to depression, social isolation, low self-esteem, self-injury, suicidal thoughts, and ongoing conflict with her sister. Deasia also had been diagnosed with high functioning autism, which made it very difficult for her to communicate with others. When we began working with her, she was about to make the transition from middle school to high school.

Through the Englewood Youth Empowerment Program/At Risk Youth Counseling services, Deasia was assisted in successfully transitioning to high school. We were able to help by working individually with Deasia and providing family counseling with her and her parents. Her depression lifted and her suicidal thoughts receded. Even though her autism continued to make relationships with peers and her family difficult, she successfully completed high school and eventually transitioned from living at home to attending a university out of state with special help from the university and a life coach.

Amanda, a single formerly homeless mother of four, was struggling, depending on child support and government assistance when she began working with a Pathway of Hope worker. As a hard worker with strong faith, she diligently pursued the goals she had developed with the worker. Having completed school only through the ninth grade, she signed up for GED classes at the corps. She had never had a job and started employment as a part-time bell ringer at Christmas.

Shortly thereafter, she was hired as the corps' part-time janitor. Attending worship services at the corps, she now is a Sunday school teacher for teen girls and helps lead the corps' Celebrate Recovery Class. Amanda completed her GED and obtained full-time employment with a good salary and health benefits. She continues to work towards goals to build a stable life for her family and a better future for her children.

John was referred to the Partner Abuse Intervention Program after pleading guilty to striking his wife with an open hand, throwing her on the bed, and smashing her car windows. When he began the program, John tended to blame his wife's "bitchiness" and lack of communication for his "loss of control." Over time, he was able to begin taking a closer look at his actions and to recognize that though he had never hit his wife before, he had engaged in a history of abusive and controlling behaviors towards her and their children.

He realized his belief that as man of the house things were supposed to be his way and that his wife's opinions were secondary. He began accepting greater responsibility for his choices, recognizing that they were attempts to establish control over his wife. He reported in group that he was implementing the skills he was learning. John acknowledged that the changes he was making were difficult and that at times he found himself still being manipulative or verbally abusive. Even though the changes he was making were beneficial to his relationship, it also meant he was not in control and as such felt vulnerable. His verbalizing the struggle appears to show effort on his part to make changes.

When there is much success, it is often because of the right combination of factors—a participant highly motivated to change his/her life, the availability of resources/opportunities, and a skilled and caring worker. As we know, not all encounters with those seeking aid lead to successful outcomes. However, we do not know when we first meet someone if the encounter will eventually lead to the participants' life being better, or if the most that will happen is the person is being listened to and being treated with dignity.

As well as feeling proud when participants make progress in their lives, we can feel good about what we do when we meet human needs as effectively as we can. Read the following by Salvation Army workers as they describe approaches with participants:

> A lot of times it works if you say, "You know, you were thinking of going in and finding out information about the CNA license. Why don't I check on that for this week and, in the meantime, why don't you apply for three jobs?" So then they do realize that you're partnering with them.

> He had been living in his RV for six weeks, and when I laid out what he would need to do to get housing, he said: "No one has ever told it to me straight before."

> She completed her Pathway of Hope goals and was doing well, then called me later when things were not going well. So now we're working on a different goal. Without the relationship we had, she was in danger of falling back into the same situation as before.

> Encouragement. Any time they meet a baby goal, little goal, take a tiny little action step—like showing up for their appointment—we try to make an emphasis, saying, "It's great that you are here," or "I'm glad to see you came today." You know, making sure everything they do is a part of what they want in the future.

In a way, each of the above descriptions by the workers can also be seen as a success story. The workers were using effective approaches and applying professional ethics, as shown in the pages of this book.

Think of *Faith in Action* as a resource for developing greater understanding of participants' situations, an aid in thinking about values, ethics, and cultural competence, and a guide to techniques and approaches the worker can use in developing a personal practice toolkit. And as we get better at what we do, we are doing our part to make The Salvation Army an even more effective force for good in the world.

CHAPTER 16

Application for Supervisors and Teams

F*aith in Action* was designed as an individual resource for workers. It also can be used by supervisors and in team meetings.

One advantage of reading a chapter at a time and discussing it later is that we focus more on what we are reading when we know we will be talking about it with others. When workers were in school, they read (or studied) material differently when they knew they would be called on to talk about it in class or would be tested on it.

But unlike when the workers were in school studying biology or algebra, the information in *Faith in Action* is directly relevant to their work with participants. As workers read the pages, they should be able to find information and techniques/approaches useful in their day-to-day work. Sharing with their co-workers what they have found useful, and listening to the ways they are applying the information in the pages of this book, can lead to more effective work with participants.

There are a number of approaches to using this book and discussing it chapter by chapter. There may be an issue, like maintaining professional boundaries, that a number of workers are dealing with. Setting up a team meeting and asking everyone to read these pages can be a starting place to discussing the issue.

The supervisor could also choose a chapter or ask for suggestions from social services staff. Once the chapter has been chosen, here are some ways to proceed:

1) The supervisor can select a particular section or approach (such as the use of affirmations on pages 74,75) and ask workers to think about their interactions with participants in recent weeks and write brief answers to the following questions before a scheduled meeting:

   Were there times you used this technique? How well did it work? Were there other situations in which this technique could have been applied? The workers will then share their answers in a team meeting.

2) The supervisor can ask workers to individually select a concept or approach in the chapter and think about how they use or could apply it. The worker should write brief answers to the following questions before a scheduled meeting:

   Were there times you used this technique? How well did it work? Were there other situations in which this could have been applied? The workers will then share their answers in a team meeting.

Because the topic of cultural competence is important and complex, team discussions on it can be helpful. Below are some specific ways in which the material in Chapter 6, Working Towards Cultural Competence, can be used:

1) After completing the "Understanding Our Social Identities" exercise (page 60), share your top three identities in pairs or in a small group. How do you reflect the importance of these identities in your interaction with others?

2) After completing the questions on page 62 (adapted from the Annie E. Casey Foundation guide to cultural and linguistic competence) in pairs or a small group compare your answers to others. How does this help you understand participants whose culture and background is different from your own?

3) Another activity for exploring identity is "Who am I?" with Eric Law: https://www.youtube.com/watch?v=lP_Ia0Zitdg. After viewing the video, take time to participate in the activity. This can then be discussed in a team meeting or training.

4) Cultural competence can be developed on a corps as well as an individual basis. This very practical checklist appraisal from the National Center for Cultural Competence can be applied and then

discussed: http://nccc.georgetown.edu/documents/ChecklistBehavioralHealth.pdf.

By interacting with other staff members about the material in this book and how the concepts and skills apply to our life and work, we gain a clearer understanding of how we can be more effective in our social services work.

PART V

References

APPENDIX A

The Salvation Army Social Services Code of Ethics

Approved by the Commissioners Conference - February 2006

The Salvation Army holds an enviable position of confidence, respect, and trust ascribed to us by the communities in which we serve and by many of the persons who participate in our holistic ministries. All programs provided by The Salvation Army encompass our Movement's mission "to preach the gospel of Jesus Christ and to meet human needs in His name without discrimination." In keeping with this mission, all staff of The Salvation Army who have responsibility for the provision of social services (officers, employees, students, and volunteers) are guided by this Code of Ethics:

A. Responsibility to Participants

Salvation Army personnel will . . .

1) Reflect in their practice the high value of each individual conferred by their Creator-God. Reflect in their practice that The Salvation Army exists for those it meets in ministry and seeks to influence the world towards the betterment of humankind.
2) Acknowledge their primary responsibility to promote the well-being of participants and their commitment to develop individual capacity for successful living.
3) Provide services for which they are appropriately educated and trained, licensed, or certified.

4) Respect the human dignity, civil and legal rights, right to self-determination, and right to informed consent of participants.

5) Strive to understand culture and how this impacts human behavior and society, being sensitive to diversity and differences in people in the development of programs and case plans for various constituencies. Staff will avoid any derogatory language or any actions that could be interpreted as harassment.

6) Advise participants about available religious services/activities with nonjudgmental inclusion, but not require their participation. Where religious participation is a program requirement there will be informed consent at the time of admission to the program.

7) Not discriminate against any participant on any basis not related to legitimate program requirements.

8) Respect participants' right to privacy and adhere to The Salvation Army Policy and Guidelines on Confidentiality and the Protection of Personal Privacy.

9) Avoid any conflict of interest that hinders the provision of service, exploits participants, or compromises The Salvation Army in any way. Staff may not engage in any business relationship with participants or their families nor accept or exchange any substantive favor, gift, or service with them.

11) Adhere strictly to established policies and standards regarding relationships and interactions with participants and their families.

12) Make referrals appropriate to participants' needs, advocating for the individual when necessary.

B. Responsibility to Colleagues

Salvation Army personnel will . . .

1) Respect all colleagues, whether supervisory or subordinate, and strive to develop a workplace environment that is supportive of the ministry of The Salvation Army, each other, and persons entering their sphere of influence.

2) Seek the advice, counsel, and support of colleagues and supervisors when necessary.

3) Accept supervisory responsibilities only when possessing or actively seeking the necessary education, skills, or training and offer responsibilities only to those who possess or are actively seeking the necessary education, skills, or training.

4) Adhere strictly to established policies and standards regarding relationships and interactions with

colleagues, especially those under their supervision.

5) Collaborate, communicate, and cooperate with other Salvation Army departments and external community resources to provide additional services for participants.

6) Discourage, prevent, confront and, as appropriate, report unethical behavior through official channels.

C. Responsibility to Society

Salvation Army personnel will . . .

1) Promote The Salvation Army's commitment to social/spiritual transformation and to the development of individual capacity to participate as a contributor to the community.

2) Promote social justice and the general well-being of the community and advocate for policies and programs that ensure all persons have access to human resources.

3) Report suspected or observed abuse of a child or vulnerable adult, criminal activity, or a threat of harm to a participant or others.

4) Assist in providing appropriate services to the community in time of public emergencies.

5) Use funds for the purposes stated. Reported program statistics will be supported by accurate program data.

D. Responsibility as Professionals

Salvation Army personnel will . . .

1) Maintain professional competence through regular continuing education, training, and supervisory feedback.

2) Maintain relationships with participants, colleagues, supervisors, and the community that are constructive, promote mutual respect, and improve the quality of service.

3) Make clear distinctions between public statements and actions as a representative of The Salvation Army from those made as a private individual. All statements made on behalf of The Salvation Army must accurately represent the official, authorized, and approved position of The Salvation Army.

4) Conduct themselves in a manner that reflects positively on The Salvation Army.

APPENDIX B

The Salvation Army Policy and Guidelines on Confidentiality and the Protection of Personal Privacy

A. Policy

People seek help from Salvation Army program units when they have special needs, which may range from fairly simple to painfully difficult. Their need for service and the help that can be given is determined through sharing factual and personal information. For this to be effective, there must be trust that the program unit will hold the shared information confidential.

Therefore, the commitment to confidentiality extends to all Salvation Army officers, employees, and volunteers. It includes the knowledge that a person is or has been a recipient of service. The Salvation Army will consider carefully matters of confidentiality as they obtain within the particular setting and commit itself to the highest level of agency practice within a given community.

The presumption of confidentiality applies to The Salvation Army unit as a whole, not only to an individual staff person, since participant information is normally shared internally for legitimate purposes of training, supervision, records accountability, and expanded client service.

Principles of confidentiality and how these are carried forward in the program unit will be part of the orientation of each new employee, advisory organization member, and other volunteers. As a general principle, no information about individuals receiving Salvation Army services will be disclosed outside the organization except when informed written consent has been obtained from the service recipient. National Salvation Army guidelines, which are received and updated periodically regarding particular confidentiality issues, should be available to all staff.

Individual program units will assume responsibility for being fully aware of and responsive to the requirements pertaining to confidentiality that impact upon them as a result of contractual commitments, the requirements of law specific to the program, the demands of standard-setting bodies, as well as Salvation Army standards for the particular program.

B. Guidelines

The following guidelines are issued in connection with The Salvation Army Policy and Guidelines on Confidentiality and the Protection of Personal Privacy.

1) *Fact of participation*

The fact that an individual is or has been a participant in a Salvation Army social services or community service program should not be disclosed outside The Salvation Army unit, except as may be specifically defined in the national standards in effect for the particular kind of program. This restraint will not apply to public meetings or programs in which participants take part as "members," e.g., troop activities, community center programs, and boys' clubs.

Inquiries by visit, telephone, or letter regarding a participant in a Salvation Army residential program should be answered with the statement that information as to whether a particular individual is or has been in residence cannot be divulged; that, if in fact the individual is in residence, he/she will be advised of the inquiry, and that, at his/her discretion, the participant will or will not communicate with the inquirer.

2) *Disclosure to other organizations*

Disclosure of limited participant information to other social services agencies, for the purpose of a referral to or from The Salvation Army, generally would be permitted if a determination is made that the disclosure is in the interest of the participant.

Before participant records can be disclosed to individuals or agencies outside The Salvation Army, the written consent of the participant must be obtained. The consent should identify the information to be disclosed, the person or agency to whom it will be disclosed, the purpose of the disclosure, and the date upon which the participant's consent expires. Use of the Authorization for Release of Information form is recommended for this purpose. The form may be found on the page following this policy.

On the other hand, information is to be withheld where The Salvation Army is required by law (as in alcohol and drug programs regulated or funded by a federal agency or in child-care or health-care facilities, which disclosure is prohibited by state regulations) and/or where by contract The Salvation Army has agreed to maintain the confidentiality of participant records.

Disclosure of information relating to participants should not be made to employers, credit agencies, unions, or other similar organizations, except under terms and conditions contractually defined where employment is an integral part of the program (e.g., contracts with federal or state correctional authorities for early release programs), or at the request and with the consent of the participant.

If there is doubt about whether participant information should be disclosed, local legal counsel should be obtained and the appropriate Salvation Army administrative headquarters should be consulted before the information is disclosed.

3) *Clearinghouse*

Whereas, as a general rule, there is no objection to participation by The Salvation Army in clearinghouses, there is any number of situations in which such disclosure is prohibited by contract or regulation or where disclosure of the information could damage the participant. Because of the varied and fluctuating makeup of the usual Army caseload, written consent of the participant should be included in the clearinghouse procedure. The information provided to the clearinghouse should be limited to that which is necessary for the clearinghouse to perform its basic function. The clearinghouse should provide some written statement (e.g., agreement or policy statement) that the clearinghouse will limit the further disclosure of such information.

Where clearinghouse information is shared electronically by several agencies through computer access, the clearinghouse should have written agreements from each participating agency limiting computer access to appropriate staff at each agency.

4) *Information to the participant*

Where required by federal, state, or local law or by a funding contract, upon written request by a participant The Salvation Army will provide such requesting participant access to information contained in his/her own case record. In other cases, The Salvation Army will consider whether such access is in the best interest of the participant and does not involve a risk of harm to others. Before allowing such access by a participant, The Salvation Army will redact information about any individuals other than the requesting participant.

If the record contains counseling records or other information relating to the participant's psychiatric, psychological, or mental health conditions, the professional responsible for the participant's treatment will review the records to determine whether the release of the information is appropriate.

If disclosure is determined not to be appropriate, the records will not be disclosed to the participant unless required pursuant to a court order. Information disclosed should be limited to that which is included in the formally completed and approved case record. The formal case record should contain only factual information and formal conclusions, not informal counselor notes and/or casual observations. Information contained in the record which was provided by other agencies or individuals, and not Salvation Army personnel, should not be disclosed to the client.

5) *Law enforcement personnel*

Except where a crime has been committed at a Salvation Army institution, disclosure to law enforcement agencies—whether local or state police, a district attorney, or the FBI—of the participation by an individual in a Salvation Army program, or of information contained in record, should be refused.

Whether served by an attorney in a civil action or at the instance of a governmental agency, a subpoena served on The Salvation Army for information regarding a participant should be resisted. It is noted that a subpoena is not the same as a court order. Specifically, local legal counsel should be retained to appear in court to move to quash the subpoena, thus compelling the person seeking disclosure of the information to show the court good cause for such disclosure, in order to request a court order. In any case, before any action is taken, the local Salvation Army operation should contact its immediate administrative headquarters.

Since an arrest warrant or a search warrant is a court order which has been issued by a court after a showing of probable cause, if such a warrant is presented to a Salvation Army facility relating to a participant in residence, The Salvation Army facility should cooperate with the law enforcement agency in making the arrest or the search, preferably in a manner which will involve the least disruption of the program at the facility.

Because law enforcement personnel are precluded from conducting a search of a residence without an arrest or search warrant, and because a criminal summons does not constitute a warrant, The Salvation Army should not produce a participant or otherwise cooperate with law enforcement personnel seeking to serve a criminal summons on a resident at a Salvation Army institution. Law enforcement personnel should be advised that they will be required to produce a valid arrest or search warrant before The Salvation Army will cooperate with them, whether in making the arrest or the search, on the terms set forth in the prior paragraph. (This paragraph added per NLC's letter of August 17, 2001.)

6) *Release of records under court order*

The Salvation Army is the owner and controller of all participant records. No records may be removed from Salvation Army premises or transmitted to other parties without specific written approval by The Salvation Army officer in charge or the executive director, in consultation with local legal counsel.

In the event that Salvation Army participant records are required by order of a court of competent jurisdiction, when good cause for such disclosure has been determined by the court, the records which have been subpoenaed by the court shall be delivered to the court, on the date requested, only by the Salvation Army officer in charge, the executive director, or other staff as designated in writing.

If the court requires a review of a participant record, the Salvation Army representative shall bring (not send) the record to the court, and request that the court review such record in closed chambers and admit only the minimum portion of such record which is relevant to the proceedings under consideration.

7) *Limitations of court testimony*

No Salvation Army personnel shall testify concerning areas of a participant's life for which they are not fully educated and licensed to make appropriate professional assessments.

8) *Child abuse*

Notwithstanding any other provisions of these guidelines, Salvation Army facilities will comply with all state and municipal laws requiring reporting to governmental agencies of instances of child abuse. Failure to comply with such laws can result in criminal sanctions.

Colonel Merle Heatwole
CHIEF SECRETARY
09/30/2013

Approved by Commissioners' Conference May 1984

Revised CC May 2000

Revised CC October 2012 and posted to National Minutes Database 7/23/2013

THE SALVATION ARMY
SAMPLE AUTHORIZATION FOR RELEASE OF INFORMATION

I, __________________a participant in The Salvation Army __________________

(Name of Participant) **(Name of Program/Service)**

hereby authorize ___________________ to disclose information about me as follows:

(Director or other employee)

Information Released **From:**	Information Released **To:**
Name:	Name:
Organization:	Organization:
Address:	Address:
Phone:	Phone

The material to be released includes:
The reason for releasing the information is:

I have had explained to me what information is to be released, to whom, and for what purpose, and I understand the explanation. By signing this form, I agree to this release of information. I understand that this release will last until (Date:) ______________, or six months from the date signed, unless I notify The Salvation Army sooner that I do not want any more information to be released or obtained.

Participant's Signature:	Date:
Witness' Signature:	Date:

APPENDIX C

Pastoral Care Plan

This *sample* pastoral care plan has been created to help corps/programs develop a pastoral care plan for their own settings. It is based on the Pastoral Care standards as stated in the Army's National Social Services Standards. Each program/corps should incorporate what they are doing/plan to do for their pastoral care program.

Purpose

The integration of pastoral/spiritual care in our social services/childcare programs is vital to fulfilling the Army's mission. Our programs are unique in the scope of services provided, and pastoral/spiritual care is integrated by intentional outreach and optional participation by program participants. The Pastoral Care Representative (PCR) is responsible for carrying out this responsibility with the involvement of staff and corps members.

The PCR is trained and experienced in providing pastoral/spiritual care in our programs. Ongoing continuing education is provided to ensure he or she is up-to-date in providing pastoral care to those in our programs.

Chaplaincy overview

The PCR works closely with social services staff to meet the Army's mission of holistic ministry. This occurs in various ways, depending on the nature of the program(s) as stated below.

The following components of pastoral care are based on the National Social Services Standards, (Chapter V, Pastoral Care Standards).

Chaplaincy to residential programs (program name)

1) As part of the initial case management process, a spiritual assessment is conducted with an intake worker or, at a later time, with the PCR. Spiritual assessments are used to determine if residents would like to be involved in the programs of the local corps or if they desire further contact with the PCR to discuss spiritual matters.
2) The National Social Service Standards indicate that a resident should have the opportunity to interact with the PCR within 72 hours after admission or at a time that is mutually agreed upon.
3) The PCR has regular communication with the staff concerning the care of the residents. This is done through referrals, staff meetings, and taking part in the clinical care meetings when appropriate.
4) Welcome baskets are given to the new residents at a time predetermined by the PCR and staff. Baskets may include personal care items as well as an invitation to corps programs.
5) Birthday parties, family fun night activities, and/or other activities take place monthly. All activities are planned with the goal of building relationships in a safe environment.
6) Pastoral counseling is made available upon request and through referral.
7) Transportation is available to corps activities for those living off-site.

Availability: The PCR has regular office hours Monday, Wednesday, and Friday mornings from 9 to noon. He or she can be contacted through Lotus Notes, email, and/or by phone. A monthly schedule is posted outside the PCR's office (by the chapel). The PCR is on call in the evening hours in the event of an emergency.

Chaplaincy to nonresidential programs (childcare program)

1) Families are given information about corps programs in their enrollment packet. They are also placed on a separate mailing list (to ensure confidentiality) if they would like to receive information about corps activities.
2) Flyers about corps activities are posted on the bulletin board in the childcare area and placed in each child's mailbox.
3) Home visits, hospital visits, and/or pastoral counseling are

provided by request.

4) The curriculum of the childcare center includes values consistent with The Salvation Army's Christian mission. The PCR and/or staff provides a time weekly for Bible stories and songs.
5) The PCR is present during events to show support for the staff and families and to form relationships with children and their parents.
6) The PCR attends childcare staff meetings with the goal of sharing information and working together to integrate the ministries of the corps and child care.

Availability: The PCR has regular office hours Monday, Wednesday, and Friday mornings from 9 to noon and during times of designated child-care activities. He or she can be contacted through email and/or by phone. A monthly schedule is posted outside the PCR's office (by the chapel). The PCR is on call in the evening hours, weekends, and holidays in the event of emergencies.

Chaplaincy to nonresidential programs (case management/Pathway of Hope)

1) Families are given information about corps programs in an informational packet. They are also placed on a separate mailing list (to ensure confidentiality) if they would like to receive information about corps activities.
2) Flyers about corps activities are posted on the bulletin board in the social services area.
3) Home visits, hospital visits, and/or pastoral counseling are provided by request.
4) The PCR is present during events to show support for the staff and families and to form relationships.
5) The PCR attends staff meetings with the goal of sharing information and working together to integrate the ministries of the corps and Pathway of Hope participants.

Availability: The PCR has regular office hours Monday, Wednesday, and Friday mornings from 9 to noon and during times of case management activities. He or she can be contacted through email and/or by phone. A monthly schedule is posted outside the PCR's office (by the chapel). The PCR is on call in the evening hours, weekends, and holidays in the event of emergencies.

Chaplaincy to personnel

The PCR attends staff meetings and participates in staff devotions. They are available to meet with staff and volunteers as requested to provide spiritual and emotional support.

Confidentiality is respected in all interactions.

Availability: The PCR is available during office hours Monday, Wednesdays, and Fridays by appointment or other times by request.

Connections with Salvation Army Corps and other churches

1) Key corps and program staff seek ways to work together through monthly management team meetings. The goal of having open communication is helpful in planning and providing ways to meet the holistic needs of those who come through our doors.
2) As appropriate the PCR's participation in the local ministerial association enhances the ability to make appropriate referrals and collaborate on events.

Documentation

1) Copies of referrals and spiritual assessments are kept in the program participant's file in a secure location. Notes of a confidential nature are kept in a locked file cabinet in the PCR's office.
2) Members of the Corps Council and Advisory Board/Council are given monthly reports of the pastoral ministry and statistics are kept.

The Salvation Army Mission Statement:

The Salvation Army, an international movement, is an evangelical part of the universal Christian church. Its message is based on the Bible. Its ministry is motivated by the love of God. Its mission is to preach the gospel of Jesus Christ and to meet human needs in His name without discrimination.

Revised 2.29.16

APPENDIX D

Position Description of the Pastoral Care Representative (PCR)

This *template* of a position description for the Pastoral Care Representative (PCR) has been created to help corps/programs identify the job duties of that individual. It is based on the Pastoral Care standards as stated in The Army's National Social Services Standards, (Chapter V, Pastoral Care Standards) and should be developed in conjunction with the pastoral care plan.

Areas of responsibility:

- Chaplaincy to Residential Programs *(delete if not applicable).*
- Chaplaincy to Nonresidential Programs *(delete if not applicable.)*
- Chaplaincy to Personnel.
- Connections with Salvation Army Corps and Other Churches.
- Documentation.

The Pastoral Care Representative reports to:

The Pastoral Care Representative's primary contact at the program(s) is:

Specific Functions:

(Functions should coincide with responsibilities as outlined in the Pastoral Care Plan and based on standard 5.2.3, include provision of religious services, visitation, Bible studies, staff support, crisis support, referral sources, facilitating/coordinating faith group involvement, making Christian literature available,

spiritual counseling and prayer, and providing spiritual assessments as appropriate to the setting.

1) Chaplaincy to Residential Programs (by program).

2) Chaplaincy to Nonresidential Programs (by program).

3) Chaplaincy to Personnel.

4) Connections with Salvation Army Corps and Other Churches.

5) Documentation

_______________________________________ ________________

Signature of Pastoral Care Representative Date

Revised 9.15.16

APPENDIX E

Spiritual Needs Assessment Tool

Contact Information

Participant's Name: ______________________ Date of Birth: _________

Address: ____

Telephone #:

(Home) ____________________ (Cell) ____________________

Services currently received from The Salvation Army:

____

____

____

Pastoral Care Representative: ______________________________

Date of Interview: ______________

Introduction

The mission of The Salvation Army is to meet the practical and spiritual needs of humanity. To that end, the following questions have been designed to help the Pastoral Care Representative address any spiritual issues of participants. This assessment tool is only a guide for conversations. It is participant-centered and is meant to create an environment of trust. You are encouraged to rely on it as a guide to open the discussion to spiritual issues, not judge.

Faith and belief

1) Do you consider yourself spiritual or religious?

____
____
____
____
____

2) Do you have spiritual beliefs that help you cope with stress or difficulties?

____
____
____
____
____
____
____
____

3) What gives your life meaning?

____
____
____
____
____
____
____
____
____

Importance of faith or belief

1) What importance does your faith or belief have in your life?

____
____
____
____
____
____
____
____
____

2) Have your beliefs influenced how you take care of yourself when experiencing difficulties?

____
____
____
____
____
____
____
____
____
____

3) What role do your beliefs play in regaining normalcy or stability in your life?

____
____
____
____
____
____
____
____

Community

1) Are you part of a spiritual or religious community?

____
____
____
____
____
____
____
____
____

2) Is your spiritual or religious community of support to you? How?

____
____
____
____
____
____
____
____
____

3) Is there a group of people who you really love or who are important to you?

____
____
____
____
____
____
____
____

Pastoral care

1) How would you like me, the pastoral care representative, to address issues that brought you to The Salvation Army?

____
____
____
____
____
____
____
____

2) How can we assist you in your spiritual care?

____
____
____
____
____
____
____
____

3) What would you like to have included in your spiritual care while you are receiving services through our facility?

____
____
____
____
____
____
____
____

4) Do you wish to share any feedback regarding the way in which our facility is meeting your spiritual needs?

____
____
____
____
____
____
____
____

5) Is there anything else that you would like to share with us to assist us in serving your spiritual needs?

____
____
____
____
____
____
____
____

Are you interested in having additional contact with the Pastoral Care Representative? Y_____ N_____

Next scheduled contact:

____

Pathway of Hope Manual, 2012

Glossary of Terms

Activity: actions the program takes to achieve desired outcomes. Some examples of activities are food distribution, counseling, case management, etc.

Advocacy: a broad-based type of problem solving designed to protect the personal and legal rights of individuals. In addition to individual advocacy, there are at least two other types of advocacy: system advocacy is used to change systems and to promote social causes, and legislative advocacy is used to change laws.

Assessments: tools that are used in the program's work with participants. Eligibility criteria is determined with an intake assessment and more in-depth work with participants takes place through the use of any number of assessments to determine strengths, sufficiency and hope. Once assessment tools are completed with a participant, goals can be set and progress monitored.

Case worker/Case manager: See Worker

Client: see Participant

Collaboration: a structured process where two or more people or organizations work together toward a common goal by sharing knowledge and building consensus.

Communities:

- **Collaborating Community:** those agencies, public and private, that provide funding to the program and/or work in coalition with the program to provide more effective services.

- **Target Community:** the persons and/or the concerns targeted for service by the program. These may be defined by socio-economic status, geographic location, gender, age and/or other program related criteria.

Consumer: see Participant

Code of Ethics: a framework that serves to guide the professional conduct of officers and staff members.

Confidentiality: the duty to maintain confidence and thereby respect privacy. Privacy relates to personal information that a person would not wish others to know without prior authorization.

Conflict Resolution: the process of attempting to resolve a dispute by listening to and providing opportunities to meet each side's needs and address their interests so that all are satisfied with the outcome.

Crisis Intervention: the methods used to offer immediate, short-term help to individuals experiencing an event that produces emotional, mental, physical, and behavioral distress or problems.

Cultural Competence: denotes a set of attitudes and skills that enable the provision of service in a manner that is sensitive, respectful and responsive to the differing backgrounds, customs, languages, values, expectations, etc. of those The Salvation Army serves. It means identifying ways of opening the door and becoming inclusive of people who might otherwise feel uncomfortable with us, or even excluded because of their differences. It calls us to go beyond statements of non-discrimination to being proactive to bridging to others. Cultural competence is not something easily or quickly achieved. It is a lifelong process that includes training, self-examination and creative responsiveness to local needs and conditions.

Divisional Headquarters (DHQ): the headquarters responsible for all Salvation Army operations within a designated geographical area.

Eligibility Criteria: predetermined requirements by which participants may receive services.

Goal: an aspect of the case/service plan whereby a participant determines what they want to accomplish by setting measurable goals and time frames. This is done in a collaborate relationship between the participant and their worker.

Health Insurance Portability and Accountability Act (HIPAA): the United States Health Insurance Portability and Accountability Act of 1996. HIPAA establishes mandatory regulations that require extensive changes to the way that health providers conduct business to ensure privacy for those receiving any type of health/behavior health care.

Indicator: targets or measurable markers that help a program monitor how much progress it has made towards meeting or achieving a particular outcome. A well-developed indicator statement should include the following components: how much, who, what and when.

Infectious Disease: a disease that is easily spread by a specific kind of contact.

Input: the materials and resources used by the program to achieve program outcomes. Examples of inputs are staff, food, utility assistance, etc.

Intake Policy: a policy statement that defines the eligibility criteria for services as well as the services to be given.

International Headquarters (IHQ): the headquarters responsible for the work of The Salvation Army worldwide.

Logic Model: a picture of how the program works. A logic model includes what you put into your program (resources), what you do (activities), and what you plan to achieve (outputs and outcomes).

Outcome: the results that the program aims to achieve. Outcomes are frequently expressed as changes in program participants' knowledge, skills, attitudes, behavior, motivation, decisions and conditions.

Outputs: the measurable products of your program. For example, the number of persons served, the number of services provided, etc.

Participant: an individual or family unit who is involved in a service or activity offered by the program.

Pastoral Care: the provision of pastoral care or chaplaincy which includes making available spiritual care and ministry to program participants, volunteers, staff and community residents as appropriate; developing a relationship of trust; providing opportunities to worship; and connecting program participants to opportunities for further spiritual development.

Pastoral Care Plan: a written strategy or design that identifies ways that a corps/program provides outreach to meet the spiritual needs of program participants. This occurs through relationship building, clinical pastoral counseling and other means.

Pastoral Care Representative/Chaplain: an officer or staff member who coordinates or provides pastoral care to individuals and/or families receiving services from The Salvation Army.

Philosophy of Care: a philosophical statement about how we work, relate to and serve participants.

Release of Information Form: written consent by a recipient of services to share his/her information with another source.

Social Worker: see Worker

Supervision: an ongoing professional relationship whereby the supervisor supports, encourages, directs and motivates staff members that report to him/her.

Worker: a case worker, case manager, social worker or other professional who provides direct services in a Salvation Army social service setting.

Bibliography

Allport, G. W. (1954). *The nature of prejudice.* Cambridge, MA: Perseus Books.

Anthony, W.A., Cohen, M.R., and Farkas, M.D. (1990). *Psychiatric Rehabilitation.* Boston: Boston University Center for Psychiatric Rehabilitation. Referenced in Rapp, C.A. (1998). *The Strengths Model: Case Management With People Suffering From Severe and Persistent Mental Illness.* New York: Oxford University Press.

Bandura, A. (1969). *Principles of behavior modification.* New York: Holt, Rinehart, and Winston, Inc.

Berg, I.K. and Miller, S. D. (1992). *Working with the problem drinker: a solution-focused approach.* New York: W. W. Norton.

Berg, I.K. (1994). *Family-Based Services: A Solution-Based Approach.* New York: W.W. Norton & Company.

Bingham, G. (1989). *The Theology of Social Work.* Address at The Salvation Army National Social Services Conference, St. Louis, MO.

Blanchard, K. and Johnson, S. (1982). *Leadership and the One Minute Manager.* New York: William Morrow and Co.

Booth, W. (1990—original 1890 text). *In Darkest England and the Way*

Out. Retrieved from www.salvationarmytexas.org/abilene/dark est-england

Booth, W. (n.d.) *Salvation soldiery. A series of addresses on the requirements of Jesus Christ's service.* London: The Salvation Army.

Boshart, R. (2013—November 15) Iowa elder abuse law changes eyed. Retrieved from http://thegazette.com/2013/ 11/15/iowa-elder-abuse-law-changes-eyed/

Bricker-Jenkins, M., (1992). Building a strengths model of practice in the public social services. In Saleebey, D. (ed.). *The Strengths Perspective in Social Work Practice.* New York: Longman.

Brohl, K. (n.d.). Social Work and Mental Health Continuing Education Utilizing Cultural Competence in Mental Health Practice.

Burgess, D., van Ryn, M., Dovidio, J., and Saha, S. (2007). Reducing Racial Bias Among Health Care Providers: Lessons from Social-Cognitive Psychology. *Journal of General Internal Medicine,* 22(6), 882-887.

Calero, H. (2005). *The power of nonverbal communication: How you act is more important than what you say.* Aberdeen, WA: Silver Lake Publishing.

Chappell, B. (2013). Number of homeless declines again, but gains aren't universal. Retrieved from http://www.npr.org/blogs/thetwoway/2013/11/21/246589487/number-of-homeless-declines-again-but-gains-arent-universal

Cheydleur, J. (1999). *Called to Counsel: Counseling Skills Handbook.* Carol Stream, IL: Tyndale Publisher.

Coates, T. (2010). The Culture of Poverty. Retrieved from http://www.theatlantic.com/personal/archive/2010/10/a-culture-of-poverty/64854/

Commoner, B. (1971). *The Closing Circle: Nature, Man,, and Technology.* New York; Alfred A. Knopf.

Community-based Learning Class (2014). Final report to Pathway of Hope Program, Wisconsin and Upper Michigan Division of The Salvation Army Central Territory, Wauwatosa, WI.

Cooper, D. (2013). Raising the Federal Minimum Wage to $10.10 Would Lift Wages for Millions and Provide a Modest Economic Boost. Electronic Policy Institute. Retrieved from http://www.epi.org/publication/raising-federal-minimum-wage-to-1010/-

Cross, T., Bazron, B., Dennis, K., and Isaacs, M. (1989). Towards a Culturally Competent System of Care: A Monograph on Effective Services for Minority Children Who Are Severely Emotionally Disturbed: Volume I. Washington DC: Georgetown University Child Development. Retrieved from http://archive.mhsoac.ca.gov/Meetings/docs/Meetings/2010/June/CLCC_Tab_4_Towards_Culturally_Competent_System.pdf

Cutshall, S. (1996). Personal Communication, August 19.

Danziger, S., and Wimer, C. (2014). *Poverty. In State of the Union: The Poverty and Inequality Report.* Stanford, CA: The Stanford Center for Poverty and Inequality.

DeJong, P. and Berg, I.K. (1998). *Interviewing for Solutions.* Pacific Grove, CA: Brooks/Cole.

Denton, R.T. (1990). The religiously fundamentalist family: Training for assessment and treatment. *Journal of Social Work Education,* 26(1), 6-14.

DiClemente, C.C. Motivational interviewing and the stages of change. In: Miller, W.R., and Rollnick, S., Eds. 1991. *Motivational Interviewing: Preparing People To Change Addictive Behaviors.* New York: Guilford Press, 191-202.

Dufault, K. and Martocchio, B.C. (1985). Symposium on compassionate care and the dying experience. Hope: its spheres and dimensions. *The Nursing Clinics of North America.*

Egan, G. (1994). *The skilled helper: a problem-management approach to helping.* Fifth Edition. Pacific Grove, CA: Brooks/Cole.

Everstine, D., and Everstine, L. (1983). *People in crisis: Strategic therapeutic interventions.* New York: Brunner/Mazel.

Farnsworth, K.E. (1981). *Integrating psychology and theology: Elbows together but hearts apart.* Washington, D.C.: University Press of America.

Felitti V.J., Anda R.F., Nordenberg D., Williamson D.F., Spitz A.M., Edwards V., Koss, M.P., Marks, J.S. Relationship of childhood abuse and household dysfunction to many of the leading causes of death in adults: The Adverse Childhood Experiences (ACE) Study *American Journal of Preventive Medicine* 1998; 14:245–258.

Fisch, R., Weakland, J.H., and Segal, L. (1983). *The tactics of change.* San Francisco: Jossey.

Frankl, V. (1963). *Man's search for meaning.* Boston, MA: Beacon Press.

Gariepy, H. (2009). *Christianity in action: The international history of The Salvation Army.* Grand Rapids, MI: Wm. B. Eerdmans Publishing.

Garland, D.R. (1991). The Role of Faith in Practice with Clients. *Social Work and Christianity.* 18(2), 75-89.

Garland, D. R., Myers, D. R., & Wolfer, T. A. (2009). Protestant Christian Volunteers in Community Social Services Programs: What Motivates, Challenges, and Sustains Their Service. *Administration in Social Work.*

Gedeon, K. (2014). New Report Says 62% of America's Jobs Pay Less than $20 per Hour. Retrieved from http:// madamenoire.com/417738/new-report-62-americas-jobs-pay-less-20/

Goldstein, H. (1984). *Creative change: A cognitive-humanistic approach to social work practice.* New York: Tavistock Publications.

Gottlieb, G. (2012). Dual Relationships and Boundary Management in Social Work Practice. Retrieved from http://www.naswwv.org/dmgnt_files/G%208%20-%20Ethics%20and%20Dual%20Relationships%202012%20PPT%20-%20Gottlieb.pdf

Gowdy, E. and Perlmutter, S. (1993) Economic Self-Sufficiency: It's Not Just Money *Affilia,* 8(4), 368-387.

Graham, Mary Ann, Kaiser, Tamara, and Garrett, Kendra J.(1998). Naming the Spiritual: The Hidden Dimension of Helping. *Social Thought,* 18(4), 49-61.

Green, R.J. (1989). *War on Two Fronts: The Redemptive Theology of William Booth.* Salvation Army Supplies: Atlanta.

Green, R.J. (2005). *The life & ministry of William Booth: Founder of The Salvation Army.* Nashville: Abingdon Press.

Hagen, J. L., & Davis, L. V. (1995). The participants' perspective on the Job Opportunities and Basic Skills Training Program. *Social Service Review,* 69, 656-678.

Hall, J.A., Carswell, C., Walsh, E., Huber, D.L., and Jampoler, J.S. (2002). Iowa case management: Innovative social casework. *So-*

cial Work, 47(2), 132-141.

Harris, J., Erbes, C., Engdahl, P., Thuras, P., Murray-Swank, N . and Grace, D. (2011). The effectiveness of a trauma focused spiritually integrated intervention for veterans exposed to trauma. *Journal of clinical psychology* 67 (4), 425-438.

Heath, C. and Heath, D. (2010). *Switch: How to Change Things When Change is Hard.* New York: Broadway Books.

Hepburn, K. (2004). *Building Culturally and Linguistically Competent Services to Support Young Children, their Families, and School Readiness.* Baltimore: Annie E. Casey Foundation.

Hepworth, D.H., Rooney, R.H., and Larson J. (1997) *Direct Social Work Practice: Theory and Skills.* Pacific Grove, CA: Brooks-Cole Publishing.

Herman, T.L. (1992). *Trauma and Recovery.* New York: Basic Books.

Herth, K. (1991). Development and refinement of an instrument to measure hope. *Scholarly Inquiry for Nursing Practice,* 5(1), 39-51.

Herth, K. (1993). Development and psychometric evaluation. *Journal of Advanced Nursing,* 17 (10), 1251-1259.

Heyer, C. (2005). Doing the Army and Getting it Right. *Caring,* 11(1), 36-37.

Hodge, D.R. (2006). A Template for Spiritual Assessment: A Review of the JCAHO Requirements and Guidelines for Implementation. *Social Work,* 51(4), 317-326.

Hodge, D. R. (2003). The Intrinsic Spirituality Scale: A new six-item instrument for assessing the salience of spirituality as a motivational construct. *Journal of Social Service Research,* 30(1), 41-61.

Hodge, D.R. (2001). Spiritual Assessment: A Review of Major Qualitative Methods and a New Framework for Assessing Spirituality. *Social Work* 46(3), 203-214.

Hong, P. Y, P., Hodge, D. R., & Choi, S. (2012b). Spirituality and self-sufficiency among low- income jobseekers, Address at the North American Association of Christians in Social Work, October 30, 2012.

Hyman, J. (2014).Employers Beware: EEOC Stepping Up Disability Discrimination Enforcement. Retrieved from http://www.workforce.com/2014/06/02/

employers-beware-eeoc-stepping-up-disability-discrimination-enforcement/

Jackson, S. (1996). Student paper: spirituality and religion. Unpublished document.

Keith-Lucas, A. (1985). *Giving and Taking Help.* Chapel Hill: University of North Carolina Press.

Kirst-Ashman, K., and Hull, G. (2012). *Understanding Generalist Practice* (6th ed.). Belmont CA: Cengage Learning.

Kisthardt, W.E. (1992). A strengths model of case management: The principles and functions of a helping partnership with persons with persistent mental illness. In Saleebey, D. (ed.). *The Strengths Perspective in Social Work Practice*. New York: Longman.

Kisthardt, W.E. and Rapp, C.A. (1992). Bridging the gap between principles and practice: Implementing a strengths perspective in case management. In Rose, S.M. (Ed.) *Case Management and Social Work Practice.* New York: Longman.

Klingensmith, M., Can those aged 45 to 64 be saved from misery in retirement? How? Retrieved from http://www.remappingdebate.org/article/can-those-aged-45-64-be-saved-misery-retirement-how

Koenig, H., King, D., and Verna, C. (2012). *Handbook of Religion and Health* (2nd ed.). New York: Oxford Press.

Krueger, A. (2014 May). Rising income inequality causing "unhealthy division in opportunities". Retrieved from http://www.huffingtonpost.com/2012/01/12/alan-krueger-income-inequality_n_1202861.html

Krull, D.S., (2001). On Partitioning the Fundamental Attribution Error: Dispositionalism and the Correspondence Bias. *Cognitive Social Psychology: The Princeton Symposium on the Legacy and Future of Social Cognition.* Gordon B. Moskowitz, Ed. Mahwah NJ: Lawrence Erlbaum Associates, p. 214.

Kuhlmann, E.G. (1999). The Idea of Social Work: Back to the Future. *Social Work and Christianity,* 26(1), 9-38.

Larkin H, Felitti VJ, Anda RF. (2011). Social work and Adverse Childhood Experiences (ACE) research: implications for practice and health policy. *Social Work in Public Health,* 29(1), 1-16.

Locke, B., Garrison, R., and Winship, J. (1998). *Generalist Social Work Practice: Context, Story, and Partnerships*. Pacific Grove, CA: Brooks-Cole.

Loewenberg, F.M. (1988). *Religion and Social Work Practice in Contemporary American Society.* New York: Columbia University Press.

Lowery, A. (2014). Changed Lives of the Poor: Better off, but far behind. Retrieved from http://www.nytimes.com/2014/05/01/business/economy/changed-life-of-the-poor-squeak-by-and-buy-a-lot.html?_r=0 lot.html?emc=edit_th_20140501&nl=todaysheadlines&nlid=28277499&_r=

Lubove, R. (1965). *The Professional Altruist: The Emergence of Social Work as a Career: 1880-1930.* Cambridge, MA: Harvard University Press.

Lum, D. (1996). *Social work practice and people of color: A process-stage approach.* Pacific Grove, CA: Brooks/Cole Publishing Company.

Office of Faith-Based and Neighborhood Programs (2015). Frequently Asked Questions. Retrieved from http://www.whitehouse.gov/administration/eop/ofbnp/faq.

McIntosh, P. (1988). *White Privilege and Male Privilege: A Personal Account of Coming To See Correspondences through Work in Women's Studies, Working Paper 189.* Wellesley, MA: Wellesley College Center for Research on Women.

Mercier, C. and Racine, G. (1995). Case management with homeless women: A descriptive study. *Community Mental Health Journal,* 31(1), 25-37.

Miller, W., and Rollnick S. (2013). *Motivational Interviewing: Helping People Change.* New York: The Guilford Press.

Mishel, L. (n.d.). Declining value of the federal minimum wage is a major factor driving inequality. Retrieved from http://www.epi.org/publication/declining-federal-minimum-wage-inequality/

Morgaine, K. and Capous-Desyllas, M. (2015). *Anti-Oppressive Social Work Practice.* Los Angeles: Sage.

National Association of Social Workers (2006). *Code of Ethics.* Retrieved from http://www.socialworkers.org/pubs/code/default.asp

National Association of Social

Workers (2012). *Dual Relationships and Boundary Management in Social Work Practice.* Retrieved from http://www.naswwv.org/dmgnt_files/G%208%20-%20Ethics%20and%20Dual%20Relationships%202012%20PPT%20-%20Gottlieb.pdf

National Association of Social Workers (2013). *Standards for Social Work Case Management.* Retrieved from http://www. socialworkers.org/practice/standards/sw_case_mgmt.asp

National Center on Cultural Competence (n.d.). *Cultural Competence Continuum.* Retrieved from http://cssr. berkeley.edu/cwscmsreports/LatinoPracticeAdvisory/Cultural%20Competence%20Continuum.pdf

National Low Income Housing Coalition, Out of Reach. 2014. Retrieved from http://nlihc.org/oor/2014.

Norcross, J., Krebs, P., and Prochaska, J. (2011). Stages of Change. *Journal of Clinical Psychology in Session,* 67(2), 143-154.

Oettingen, G. (2014). *Rethinking Positive Thinking: Inside the New Science of Motivation.* New York: Penguin.

Office of Faith-Based and Neighborhood Programs (2015). Frequently Asked Questions. Retrieved from https://www.whitehouse.gov/administration/eop/ofbnp/faq

Okun, B.F. (1992). *Effective helping: Interviewing and counseling techniques* (4th ed). Pacific Grove, CA: Brooks-Cole. Referenced in Dejong, P. and Berg, I.K. (1998). *Interviewing for Solutions.* Pacific Grove, CA: Brooks-Cole.

Pellebon, D.A. and Anderson, C.S. (1999). Understanding the Life Issues of Spiritually-Based Clients. *Families in Society,* 87(3), 229-238.

Peres, J., Moreira-Almeida, A., Nasello, A.G., and Koenig, H.G. (2006). Spirituality and resilience in trauma victims. *Journal of Religion and Health,* 46(3), 343-350.

Pew Hispanic Center (2013). *A Nation of Immigrants.* Retrieved from http://www.pewhispanic.org/2013/01/29/a-nation-of-immigrants/

Pipher, M. (1996). *The shelter of each other.* New York: Random House.

Prochaska, J.O. and DiClemente, C.C. (1982). Transtheoretical therapy: Towards a more integrative model of change. *Psychotherapy: theory, research and practice,* 19: 276-288.

Putman, R. (2000). *Bowling Alone: The Collapse and Revival of American Community.* New York: Simon & Schuster

Rapp, C.A. (1998). *The Strengths Model: Case Management with People Suffering from Severe and Persistent Mental Illness.* New York: Oxford University Press.

Reamer, F. (1993). *Ethical dilemmas in social services.* New York: Columbia University Press.

Rommell, R. (2014 May). Drinking deeply ingrained in Wisconsin's culture. Retrieved from http://www.jsonline.com/news/wisconsin/31237904.html

Rosengren, D. (2009). *Building Motivational Interviewing skills: A practitioner workbook.* New York: The Guildford Press.

Rothman, J. (1989). Client self-determination: untangling the knot. *Social Service Review,* 63(4), 598-612.

Ryan, W. (1971). *Blaming the Victim.* New York: Random House.

Ryan-Bailey, V. (1996). The Lodge was our salvation. *The War Cry,* February 17, 20-21.

Saleebey, D. (1996). The strengths perspective in social work practice: Extensions and cautions. *Social Work,* 41, 296-305.

Saleebey, D. (1997). *The Strengths Perspective in Social Work Practice.* (4th ed.) White Plains, NY: Longman.

Sandfort, J. (1999). The Structural Impediments to Human Service Collaboration: Examining Welfare Reform at the Front Lines. *Social Service Review,* 73(3), 314-339.

Seltser, B. and Miller, D. (1993). *Homeless families: The struggle for dignity.* Urbana, IL: The University of Illinois Press.

Sheafor, B. W., Horejsi, C. R., and Horejsi, G. A. (1994). *Techniques and guidelines for social work practice,* 4th Ed. Boston: Allyn and Bacon.

Short, Kathleen (2013). The Research Supplemental Poverty Measure 2012. United States Census Population Report P60-247. Retrieved from http://www.census.gov/prod/2013pubs/p60-247.pdf

Shulman, L. (1999). *The skills of helping individuals, families, and small groups* (4th ed.). Itasca, IL: F. E. Peacock Publishers, Inc.

Smith and Hammons, S. (1979). Faith and practice: A critical integration. *Social Work and Christianity* 18(1), 1991, 6-28.

Snyder, C. R., Harris, C., Anderson, J. R., Holleran, S. A., Irving, L. M., Sigmon, S. T., Yoshinobu, L., Gibb, J., Langelle, C., & Harney, P. (1991). The will and the ways: Development and validation of an individual-differences measure of hope. *Journal of Personality and Social Psychology,* 60, 570-585.

Snyder, C.R, Rand, K.L., and Sigmon, D.R. (2002). Hope theory: A member of Positive Psychology family In *Handbook of Positive Psychology,* C.R. Snyder and Shane Lopez, eds. New York. Oxford Press.

Southern Education Foundation. (2015). Low income students now a majority in our nation´s public schools. Retrieved from http://www.southerneducation.org/Our-Strategies/Research-and-Publications/New-Majority-Diverse-Majority-Report-Series/A-New-Majority-2015-Update-Low-Income-Students-Now

Sprenkle, D.H. (1987). Treating a sex addict through marital sex therapy. *Family Relations,* 36, 11-14.

Stiegel, L.A. (1995). *Recommended Guidelines for State Courts Handing Cases Involving Elder Abuse.* Washington, DC.: National Criminal Justice Reference Service.

Swidler, A.(1986). Culture in action: Symbols and strategies. *American Sociological Review,* 51(2), 273-286.

Tajfel, H. and Turner, J. C. (1986). The social identity theory of inter-group behavior. In S. Worchel and L. W. Austin (eds.), *Psychology of Intergroup Relations.* Chicago: Nelson-Hall

Tax Policy Center (2014). Taxation and the Family : What is the Earned Income Tax Credit? Retrieved from http://www.taxpolicycenter.org/briefing-book/what-earned-income-tax-credit-eitc

The Salvation Army Central Territory (2012). *Pathway of Hope Training Manual.* Des Plaines, IL

Trattner, W. (1999). *From Poor Law to welfare state: A history of social welfare in America.* New York:

The Free Press.

U.S. Bureau of Labor Statistics. (March 2014). Characteristics of Minimum Wage Workers, 2013. Retrieved from http://www.bls.gov/opub/reports/minimum-wage/archive/characteristics-of-minimum-wage-workers-2014.pdf

U.S. Census. (2014 May) American Fact Finder. *2012 Population Estimates.* Retrieved from http://www.census.gov/acs/www/data/data-tables-and-tools/american-factfinder/

Van Hook, M.P. Incorporating Religious Issues in the Assessment Process with Individuals and Families in Hugen, B. (1998). *Christianity and Social Work: Readings on the Integration of Christian Faith and Social Work Practice.* Botsford, CT: North American Association of Christians in Social Work.

Vroom, V. (1965). *Motivation in Management.* New York, NY: American Foundation for Management Research.

Vygotsky, L.S. (1978). *Mind in Society: The Development of Higher Psychological Processes.* Cambridge, Massachusetts: Harvard University Press.

Wagner, S. L., & Herr, T. (1995). *Understanding case management in a welfare-to-work program: The Project March perspective.* Chicago: Project Match--Families in Transition Association.

Wallace, J.R. (1998). *Faith-Based Casework: Towards a Synthesis Model for Social Work Practice.* Address at The Salvation Army Social Services Seminar, Stephens Point, WI.

Wallis, J. (1994). *The Soul of Politics.* New York: New Press and Orbis Books.

Waters, D. B. and Lawrence, E. C. (1993). *Competence, courage, and change: an approach to family therapy.* New York: W. W. Norton and Company.

Weick, A. and Saleebey, D. (1998). Postmodern Perspectives for Social Work. *Christianity and Social Work,* 18(3), 21-40.

Weinberg, K. (2014). Personal Communication, November 16.

Willis, J. and Todrov, A. (2006). First impressions: Making up your mind after a 100-ms exposure to a face. *Psychological Science,* 17(7), 592-598.

Wright, S. C. (2009). Cross-group contact effects. In S. Otten, T.

Kessler & K. Sassenberg (Eds.), *Intergroup relations: The role of emotion and motivation* (pp. 262–283). New York, NY: Psychology Press.

Winship, J. (2014a). *Students' Perceptions and Practice Reflections.* Unpublished document.

Winship, J. (2014b). *Community Context.* Unpublished manuscript.

Scripture

KJV - King James Version;
LB-Living Bible;
MEV - Modern English Version;
NIV - New International Version;
NKJV-New King James Version;
Phillips, J.B.

CPSIA information can be obtained
at www.ICGtesting.com
Printed in the USA
LVHW07s1106140418
573326LV00005B/6/P

9 780964 83475